By the same author:
 I Am Joseph
 I Am Jeremiah

I am Moses

ALAN PAIN

Illustrations by Sue Lea

KINGSWAY PUBLICATIONS
EASTBOURNE

Copyright © Alan Pain 1991.
The right of Alan Pain to be identified as author of this work
has been asserted by him in accordance with the Copyright,
Design and Patents Act 1988.

First published 1991.

All rights reserved.
No part of this publication may be reproduced or
transmitted in any form or by any means, electronic
or mechanical, including photocopy, recording, or any
information storage or retrieval system, without
permission in writing from the publisher.

Biblical quotations are from the
New International Version © 1973, 1978, 1984
by the International Bible Society.
Anglicisation © 1979, 1984 by Hodder and Stoughton Ltd

Front cover illustration by Taffy Davies

British Library Cataloguing in Publication Data

Pain, Alan
I am Moses.
I. Title
222.12092

ISBN 0 86065 724 8

Printed in Great Britain for
KINGSWAY PUBLICATIONS LTD
1 St Anne's Road, Eastbourne, E Sussex BN21 3UN by
Richard Clay Ltd, Bungay, Suffolk
Typeset by Watermark, Crostwight, Norfolk

To
Eric, Derek, Colin
and, more recently, Donald;
full-time colleagues whose loyal friendship
is given far more than
it is deserved.

Contents

	Introduction	7
1.	My Unlikely Start	9
2.	Reluctant to Serve God	23
3.	Let My People Go	35
4.	The Way Out – Exodus	50
5.	My Father-in-Law	64
6.	The Challenge of Partnership	79
7.	Coping with Complaints	96
8.	Coping with Myself	113
9.	Our Experience of God	128
10.	Worship	143
11.	The Ten Commandments	159
12.	The Mountain and the Desert	174
	Postscript	185

Introduction

Richard Attenborough's compelling film *Cry Freedom* includes a song honouring great names and significant places which 'cry freedom' for South Africa: Mandela, Sisulu, Stephen Biko; Soweto, Sharpeville, Mamelodi and many others.

Moses was the original great name who cried freedom – for Israel. The assurance he received from God (Ex 3:7–9), and the plea he made to Pharaoh, 'Let my people go' (Ex 5:1), give a biblical inspiration to the modern demand for freedom from the demonic tyranny of racial oppression. The same assurance and the same plea of Moses inspire that scourge of cautious orthodoxy, liberation theology. As if Jesus had no concern for human freedom (Lk 4:16–21).

I Am Moses is the third in a series of imaginary biblical autobiographies. Like its two predecessors, *I Am Joseph* and *I Am Jeremiah*, it has a dual purpose: to persuade you to read the Bible, and to help you enjoy it. Inside those dusty, unread pages of Scripture lie stories which are tremendously exciting and frequently funny, although you may need help to dig out the humour. (What do you think actually happened when frogs flooded Egypt, and what if they appeared in similar numbers today?) But these stories also penetrate a generation which has become as superficial as it is sophisticated, and we need confidence in our message.

If you don't see the life of Moses in the same way as I do, I'm happy to live with our disagreement provided you move on from this book to the Bible, the most interesting, powerful, and important book of all. God will meet you in your reading; he will make it time well spent, and I shall be satisfied.

1
My Unlikely Start

You probably know a great deal about me, before I tell you anything, which gives you a big advantage from the start, but the opportunity to speak for myself has eluded me for years and I'm not letting it slip now. All I ask is that you give me a fair hearing because I have no dispute with our official records. They have proved tremendously helpful in confirming minor details for me, but you can't beat a story which comes straight from the horse's mouth – whose name, this time, is Moses, the son of Levite parents (Ex 2:1).

My early days were distinctly unpromising, but three separate events exercised a profound influence on the course of my life: an Egyptian princess adopted me and we became a single-parent family living in her father's palace; I was publicly exposed as a murderer and fled the country; God summoned me to return to Egypt to lead the miraculous escape he was planning for our slave nation. Now, years later, I am an old man with little time left, so let's get on with the story.

Before I was born, the Egyptian Pharaoh took steps to destroy our Hebrew race. We're far from delicate creatures who can't breed in captivity. We're a tough lot, and we had multiplied in slavery. Never a brave man unless the odds were heavily stacked in his favour, Pharaoh was alarmed by our mushrooming birthrate, fearing that sheer numbers would give us the courage to rebel against him. He issued brief instructions, and you didn't need too many brains to understand his intentions. 'Every boy that is born you must throw into the river, but let every girl live' (Ex 1:22). Did he really think Hebrew parents would take that lying down? We may not be advanced enough to scan the womb to learn when a boy is on the way, but we know what to do when one arrives. Whenever the news flashed round our emergency grapevine, 'It's one with a spout,' a secret network sprang into action, and no Egyptian understood our Hebrew word for 'spout'. That baby boy may not be your son, but one day your daughter would be looking for a husband, and good men were likely to be thin on the ground. We were all in this together, and my mum was not the only one who refused to offer her son's premature obituary, 'Drowned at birth in loyal obedience to Pharaoh.' We saved hundreds of boys, but tragedies of discovery and murder abounded, usually the grim result of betrayal by sly informers, and we acted with instant severity if we caught them at work. Wouldn't you have done the same if your son was at stake?

My mother kept me at home for a few weeks, but she soon reached the point where she could no longer conceal me and she hid me in the local river where the eagle eye of the Egyptian princess quickly spotted me. Her attendants carried me back to the royal palace, and the Pharaoh's daughter readily adopted me as her own son. From all I gathered later, she was a very indulged young lady, but I can't complain about the way she treated me. My new mother was happy for my Hebrew family to be my nursemaids, although she never suspected they were anything more than worthless Hebrew slaves with nothing better to do than drool over the helpless infant they attended so faithfully each day.

Years later, I chanced across an Egyptian thrashing

one of my own people. Wrongly assuming that no one was watching, I killed the foreign bully. The next day I found two Hebrews brawling and I tried to intervene, always a risky business. It was a bad mistake on my part, and they rounded furiously on me as one of them spelt out in no uncertain terms that he'd seen the savage punishment I had meted out the previous day. 'Are you thinking of killing me as you killed the Egyptian?' (Ex 2:14). That put me into a flat spin, and I panicked. Pharaoh's flapping ears soon picked up the news, and I took the only option left to me; I ran for it, fleeing Egypt for the nearest desert. I went to live in Midian (Ex 2:15).

I determined never to return to Egypt. My adoptive mother had been good to me, but if she wanted to see me again she could travel outside Egypt to a place where I could guarantee my immunity from the deadly intentions of her father. I never did call him 'Grandpop'. But things change quickly when God steps in, as you must have discovered for yourself. They changed for me in a shattering experience of his presence in which he confronted me with his demand on my life. He told me to go back to Egypt. There was no misunderstanding him, although I tried hard. 'So now go. I am sending you to Pharaoh to bring my people the Israelites out of Egypt' (Ex 3:10). If you were in my position, is that what you'd want to hear? No, and neither did I. I wasted no time in mustering my defences: the call is too hard, the errand is futile, and I'm a useless speaker when the job requires a man of rare eloquence.

If it needed a long time to persuade God to call someone else, that was fine by me. He must appreciate what a mistake it was to choose me, and I intended to keep up my protests for as long as necessary. Of course, my excuses cut no ice with God, and my desperate reluctance left him firmly unmoved – in fact, he didn't turn a hair. There's no point in denying that the mere thought of returning to Egypt terrified me – how would you have felt in my place? – and I determined to escape

God. He was offering a job I didn't want, and his blunt refusal to negotiate easier terms frightened me. I thought my excuses were foolproof, but if you've concluded that I was wasting my time, you're about right. We always waste our time when we attempt to refuse God. Since then, my life's been a mixture of great privilege and extreme difficulty, and I'm no different from other leaders who expect sympathy for their heavy responsibilities but refuse to delegate leadership to frustrated partners.

If you had to do it in one word, how would you define my role in Israel? Was I a king? Certainly, I have given laws, administered justice, chosen the route for our wilderness journey and supervised the way we organise our tribal life – all of which are functions of kingship. But I have not led Israel into battle and I've made no arrangements for my son to succeed me. Can you imagine any self-respecting monarch failing to make careful provision for his son to follow him, to say nothing of an ambitious queen whose maternal instincts would see to it that her son succeeded his father? No, I was not a king in Israel.

Was I a priest? I'm sure that's how many people will remember me, because the law I received from God and handed on to the people included instructions for the sanctuary and the forms of our worship. That is priestly work by any standards. But if you expect anything from a priest, you want him to offer the appointed sacrifices at the right time on the right day. I have not done that, preferring to leave it to Aaron, the Levites, and carefully chosen young men, acting deliberately on the instructions God gave me. 'Anoint Aaron and his sons and consecrate them so that they may serve me as priests' (Ex 30:30). 'Then he sent young Israelite men, and they offered burnt offerings and sacrificed young bulls as fellowship offerings to the Lord' (Ex 24:5).

To be honest, I don't see the point of this concern to define my role, and I object to any conclusion which squeezes me into a single mould. But I've no doubt that the debate will reopen with renewed enthusiasm when I've gone, as scholarly argument thrives on its own disagreements. If you are the pioneer of a nation which emerges with a unique religious experience, and if you have been the dominant figure in its national life for many years, you must have fulfilled all sorts of roles which future generations will prefer to separate into neatly defined categories. None of these is adequate to describe what I have been for Israel. You can highlight my experience of God, my forty days on the mountain and my delivery of divine decisions, concluding that this justifies pinning on me the label 'seer'. But, as with the titles 'king' and 'priest', vital ingredients of the seer's work are missing from my leadership. I have neither offered miraculous knowledge of the future nor given clairvoyant explanations of mystical secrets, a practice I particularly detest. In short, I have never been a seer.

Let me tell you what I think. If you are determined to find a single definition for me, one that is more explicit than 'leader', my suggestion is that you remember me as a 'prophet'. My recent assurance to Israel was clear enough: 'The Lord your God will raise up for you a prophet like me from among your brothers. You must listen to him' (Deut 18:15). A prophet is someone who speaks out what he believes God has told him to say, and I have done that. If that has meant calling a spade a spade, I have not hesitated. Everyone knows where he stands with me. God called me to declare his word, and he gave me a definite job to do. I have spent my life in obedience to him, taking the rough with the smooth from the beginning when he spoke forcefully to me: 'So now go. I am sending you to Pharaoh to bring my people the Israelites out of Egypt.... When you have brought the people out of Egypt, you will worship God on this mountain' (Ex 3:10,12).

This book describes the mountains and valleys I have faced as leader of Israel. God called our nation into being through the Exodus rescue from Egypt, and he gave us a name to use when we spoke of him. His original summons imposed an obligation on me which he has not yet lifted, and I haven't retired – you don't collect a pension in the desert. Since then, our circumstances have often suggested the end of the road for Israel, but God never leaves a job half-done – there is no end to a road he has laid. You will read of our suffering as slaves and our miraculous escape. It's up to you to decide whether you view that escape as an amazing quirk of nature or the supernatural effect of God's word. After all, the sea doesn't roll back every day, not even in the most violent wind. Read on, and you'll follow a difficult wilderness journey which our irritable moods made notoriously tedious. It brought me to the brink of despair and the edge of the new land which God has promised us: Canaan.

Here is more than the mere history of Israel; here is the marvellous way in which God has fulfilled three mighty promises which offered us our dreams – deliverance, spiritual adoption, and a land of our own. 'Therefore, say to the Israelites: "I am the Lord and I will bring you out from under the yoke of the Egyptians. I will free you from being slaves to them and will redeem you with an outstretched arm and with mighty acts of judgement. I will take you as my own people, and I will be your God...I will bring you to the land I swore with uplifted hand to give to Abraham, to Isaac and to Jacob. I will give it to you as a possession. I am the Lord"' (Ex 6:6–8).

No nation can afford to be casual in the defence of its territory. It views every threat of invasion, let alone the seizure of its land, as an unmitigated disaster to be resisted at all costs. We are no different from any other people who stop at nothing to protect their land, and we were more than willing to serve a God who assured us of the country for which we had longed.

Now that I have set the scene for you, we can return to the beginning when the Israelites were in Egypt. Many years previously, we had followed Joseph's family to a land of plenty in a world of scarcity, but the tide turned against us. Joseph's generation disappeared, the Israelites multiplied, and our numbers became much more of a serious threat to Egypt than a welcome source of cheap labour. A Pharaoh rose to power who neither knew Joseph nor cared for his memory. He was more than willing to listen to the cunning whispers of those who plotted to destroy the despised immigrants, and he set in motion his own policy. 'Look,' he said to his people, 'the Israelites have become much too numerous for us. Come, we must deal shrewdly with them or they will become even more numerous and, if war breaks out, will join our enemies, fight against us and leave the country' (Ex 1:10). That was not the first time a vicious minority oppressed an enslaved majority because it was too afraid and too selfish to forego its unwarranted privileges and allow them their basic rights, and it won't be the last time. Many more people will cry for their freedom as we cried for ours. Pharaoh imposed a terrible form of compulsory family planning on Israel, and I was born into the generation of his intended victims.

Pharaoh's plan was simple and in two parts, but the first part didn't work. He oppressed us, but we multiplied. 'So the Egyptians came to dread the Israelites and worked them ruthlessly. They made their lives bitter with hard labour' (Ex 1:12–13). Someone should have reminded the stupid man that if you treat people that badly, the only pleasure you leave them in life is breeding babies.

The second part of his plan was worse. He issued precise orders to the Hebrew midwives to regulate, and ultimately to obliterate Israel. 'When you help the Hebrew women in childbirth...if it is a boy, kill him; but if it is a girl, let her live' (Ex 1:16). Now, it's important for you to realise that our midwives know their job. They are skilled professionals with vast experience of harsh conditions. Furthermore, Pharaoh picked on two of the biggest jokers we had at the time, Shiprah and Puah. They listened attentively to him, nodded quietly in a pretence of agreement, smiled to themselves, and ignored his instructions. 'The midwives...feared God and did not do what the king of Egypt had told them to do; they let the boys live' (Ex 1:17).

It's an awful pity that men can't give birth, because these two women would have had a field day with Pharaoh if he had ever gone into labour. They were itching to get their hands on his wife, but he was the one they really wanted. Alas, the stronger sex is too frail to cope with childbirth, and Pharaoh escaped the clutches of Shiprah and Puah, formidable ladies of Israel. How ironic that this great ruler had nothing better to do with his time than interfere with the daily work of foreign midwives. As a thwarted leader you'd expect him to avenge himself by regrading the offending professionals – the usual tactics of petty tyrants – but he preferred to confront them with their disobedience.

Whatever you do, never underestimate the female sense of humour which can be as cunning as it is subtle. When Pharaoh summoned them to his palace, Shiprah and Puah went to town on him with a malicious knock at the pampered Egyptian women they had watched with amused contempt. We're a tough nation, and our mothers-to-be don't miss their relaxation classes, even in captivity. The benefits are obvious once they are in labour, and there is no song or dance when these resilient ladies give birth. They grunt, but they do not shriek. Only a foreign king, and a mere male at that, would fall for the mischievous explanation our midwives served up for Pharaoh. 'Hebrew women are not like Egyptian women; they are vigorous and give birth before the midwives arrive' (Ex 1:19). God smiled at the joke, it was his kind of humour, and Israel continued to increase (Ex 1:20). Pharaoh wasn't usually slow on the uptake, and it dawned on him that two women had made a fool of him. A typical man, he lost his temper and exacted brutal revenge in a murderous edict which served as a grim welcome to me, baby Moses: 'Every boy that is born you must throw into the river' (Ex 1:22).

My birth was therefore a furtive affair. We sent out no announcement cards and we received none, which may not have been a bad thing because most of the words they contain are worse than stupid. In my mum's eyes I was a beautiful baby, an impartial judgement which I warmly applaud (Ex 2:2). She nursed me at home for three months, knowing all the time that these idyllic days were strictly numbered. The threat hanging over me tortured her as she dressed me each day in bright pink, dreading all the time that anyone would walk in while she was changing my nappy. Informers, well paid for their willing treachery, were always on the prowl to spare Pharaoh the expense of an official police force.

Did Pharaoh seriously believe that any mother would drown her own son? Can you think of a mother who would do that? Oh, I know that some of you have been sorely tempted as your son grew older, but that's different. Wringing the neck of a naughty boy is not the same as drowning him at birth. My mum decided to place me in the water, fulfilling the letter but not the spirit of Pharaoh's wicked command. 'She got a papyrus basket...and coated it with tar and pitch' (Ex 2:3).

You do not have to be a parent to appreciate what my family suffered. Our ordeal was part of the national plight – we Hebrews were in it together – but that was cold comfort to my parents who longed for another son. They loved their daughter, Miriam, but they yearned for boys, and boys were under threat. Aaron was now three years old, and they didn't want to breed daughter after daughter until another boy arrived. Husband and wife prayed anxiously for a son, but they were not getting any younger. Their prayer was simple, 'Lord teach us patience, but give us a son now.' I was the answer to their fervent prayers, and they vested parental ambitions as much in me as in Aaron. But cruel masters plotted to destroy these hopes before their very eyes.

I doubt if I was any healthier than the next baby, but their awful predicament persuaded my parents that I was unusually robust. Mum enjoyed an easy pregnancy with me and a trouble-free labour, telling me later that I walked very early. You will realise that masters don't allow pregnant slaves to use maternity wards with expensive equipment, and that's how it was with us. Our women still make do with two stones set slightly apart where they sit at the moment of delivery. Trained midwives may be available to help them, but other women are at hand to make excellent assistants. Immediately after its birth, we rub a baby with salt, wrapping the infant in swaddling cloths. Mother often chooses the name for her latest offspring, although family discussions typical of many cultures will give the subject a good airing with the usual arguments, jokes, and howls of disbelieving protest.

Leah named Reuben; Rachel named Joseph, and, as she died giving birth, she named her second son Ben-Oni, which her husband Jacob subsequently altered to Benjamin (Gen 29:32; 30:24; 35:18). Occasionally Dad muscles in on the action, using his traditional authority which most wives manage to tame in the privacy of their own home. Abraham named Hagar's son Ishmael, and it was God rather than Sarah who instructed him to call their son Isaac (Gen 16:15; 17:19). I had my own way with my son, naming him Gershom in recognition of the fact that I had been a *ger* at the time of his birth, an alien living in a foreign land (Ex 2:22). The circumstances of a child's birth often provide the inspiration for its name. My Egyptian mother named me 'Moses', saying, 'I drew him out of the water' (Gen 4:1; Ex 2:10). Your name is not so bad after all, is it?

Only a fool could seriously believe that I would lie undetected in the water for long. My family had their heads screwed on the right way; they were buying time in their frantic search for a good idea to save my life. I was far from a placid baby, but my parents knew the story of Joseph well enough to hope that God would once again act in power to protect a young man with a big future. I was blissfully unaware of their agony, loving every minute of my prolonged bath as the water gently rocked my improvised cradle, and the ducks peered in, curious about this strange newcomer.

Pharaoh's daughter often came to bathe in this stretch of water. Her attendants kept guard for prying eyes because the princess was a beautiful young woman, and few men would refuse the chance to watch her. When you're only three months old such exciting opportunities don't interest you, and I gave a good yell which attracted the attention I wanted and my mother dreaded. My guess is that she was staking everything on the maternal instincts of the princess whose bathing habits were well known. Mum had conceived a desperate plan, and her shrewd calculations were accurate, as you'd expect of a good Hebrew. The princess herself found me, and her female compassion easily overcame her racial prejudice. 'She saw the basket among the reeds and sent her slave girl to get it. She opened it and saw the baby. He was crying, and she felt sorry for him. "This is one of the Hebrew babies," she said' (Ex 2:5–6).

My sister was nearby, reacting to every movement as intently as a lioness stalks her unsuspecting prey. This was the chance she wanted. She rushed in with an immediate offer of voluntary nursing and raced off to fetch my mother, who hid her delight with a convincing display of total surprise. The Egyptians were happy to pay her child benefit for nursing her own son: 'Take this baby and nurse him for me, and I will pay you' (Ex 2:9). (We Hebrews do land on our financial feet, don't we?) And so an Egyptian princess adopted me, willingly paying my mum to be my nanny, albeit a temporary appointment (Ex 2:10).

MY UNLIKELY START

I can't tell you much about my childhood or my early teens. They represent hidden years, and I won't be the only religious leader whose early years frustrate the search for details which are lost for ever. In my case, they would prove an unhelpful distraction from the essential story, and you should not regret their loss. My upbringing made it inevitable that I would learn the Egyptian language, and I soon spoke it like a native. Despite my commendable fluency, I knew it was a foreign tongue; foreign because of the blood which flowed in my veins, and foreign through the purpose God held in store for me.

My adoption was not a secret. The truth was not kept from me, nor would the attempt have succeeded when many people had a shrewd, if unofficial idea of the story. I spent years of unrecorded anonymity in Egypt, a stranger welcomed in high places with his heart elsewhere. No one accused me of being an 'alien', and no one risked poking fun at me. I was too strong and my royal family too powerful for me to concede the upper hand to ridicule. In my heart I belonged to the Hebrews, even before I learned the whole story, and that made me willing to accept, even to welcome, an aloof isolation in Egypt. I felt something I could not put into words: a future lay before me, far beyond my existing horizons; a future I didn't want, and a future which would be bad news for Egypt. I waited to know more, but it caught me unwilling as well as unawares when the time came.

In my teens I did struggle with the knowledge of my adoption. The torment worsened when I discovered my Hebrew family, and I understood how dangerous it would be for them if the full truth leaked out. Deep down, I valued my adoptive mother, in fact I loved her. She had saved my life by bringing me into the protection of Egyptian royalty, an amusing irony since her own father had issued the decree which should have snuffed me out at birth. At the time, I longed to feel the same as other children and to grow up with my own people. I rebelled against the circumstances which made that impossible, committing myself to change things when I was older. In my greatest need of security, I was insecure. A puzzling affinity existed with my Hebrew nanny long before I realised she was my mother. It unsettled me until I understood who she really was. Fortunately, my adoption has not wounded me or scarred me for life, and the strange upbringing I received in Egypt provoked strong convictions about parenthood which I hope have benefited my own children. But that's not for me to say; you must ask them what they think.

2

Reluctant to Serve God

It was a day which began like any other, with no hint of what was to come. You know the kind of day I mean, don't you? It dawns with no indication that it will be anything except ordinary, but it throws up a totally unexpected drama.

I woke up that morning a shepherd, anxious to avoid the scorching heat by taking my father-in-law's sheep as far as the hill country of Horeb, later known as 'the mountain of God' (Ex 3:1; 1 Kings 19:8). I went to bed that night an ex-shepherd, the newly commissioned national leader summoned by God to return to Egypt to head up Israel's escape from captivity. The Lord met me in a terrifying moment; well, he intended a moment, but I spun it out with lengthy protests and persistent questions. It was rather like those biscuits you bake as melting moments but which turn out to be solid half-hours.

God interrupted my jobs for the day with an amazing summons which I now label 'my call'. He set me a task I didn't want, and for which I would not have applied if he had advertised the vacancy; I would have drawn it to the attention of more suitable friends. I suppose I must have some natural qualities of leadership, but I showed no early indication of a born leader destined to rise to the top. I had renounced my opportunity to live in Egyptian luxury when I fled the country, wanting nothing more than a backstage role without awkward enquiries into my violent past.

The more I reflect on that call, the more I see how quickly it changed the entire course of my life. Its initial impact and its continuing power stopped me resigning in times of deep discouragement and kept me humble in rare moments of success. An awareness of the call of God will become a normal part of the experience of those to whom he entrusts great responsibility. Many of them will provide a graphic account of their call, and we shall value their spiritual integrity as well as their fascinating variety, but sometimes they will prefer to keep it to themselves, relying on their public ministry as sufficient evidence of God's initiative in their lives.

Whatever you do, don't treat all those who come after me as if they have to fit into the mould of my experience of God. I am telling you what happened to me, but it will be different for you. God treats us as individuals, doing what is necessary to persuade us to obey him, although many of us give him a hard time. He doesn't call us so that we can flaunt our experience over those who have not met him as we have, and we should not compel a man or woman to follow the pattern which the Lord made for us, but not for them.

I found a bush on fire. This was nothing unusual, for in times of drought bush-fires often happen. It only becomes dangerous if a sudden gust of wind catches hold of the blaze. This time there was not even a breeze, and I felt no immediate alarm. The fire would peter out with no more damage than the loss of a lone bush from the hilly desert.

But this was no ordinary fire. Don't ask me how I knew that, because I can't tell you; it was that inexplicable spiritual instinct which we learn slowly to trust. The fire was burning for my benefit. What I saw with my own eyes, I also felt in my spirit; something was happening in the unseen world which concerned God and me, but no one else. Nature was no more than an interested spectator of our meeting. The fire did not frighten me but I was tense, creeping closer to the burning bush, not for its warmth but under an inner compulsion to be involved. A voice called me, 'Moses, Moses' (Ex 3:4), but you would have heard nothing. You may think that's nonsense, but I suspect you understand perfectly well what I'm driving at. This encounter had no meaning for anyone but me. My reply to the one who called my name was deceptively calm because I was trembling inside, 'Here I am' (Ex 3:4). Would you have come up with a better answer, especially when you knew there was no point in hiding?

There are rare occasions, only a handful for each of us, when God bursts in with a vivid clarity which we later describe as 'the glory of God'. These high points of spiritual certainty help us realise why others talk about 'the fear of the Lord'. We mislead people if we give the impression that 'the fear of the Lord' means hiding in the corner whenever God comes, in case he tramples us underfoot. For me, 'the fear of the Lord' is the expression of my awareness of God's fiery presence and mighty word. The experience before the burning bush when God commanded me to remove my shoes because I was standing on holy ground (Ex 3:5), evoked just such a response. Tomorrow I could trample the grass with my boots and my sheep, but today the Lord pronounced it 'holy', and that meant bare feet for me, which the sheep already had. This was a warning I did not violate.

If you are an impatient reader, you will be itching to hurry on to the excitement of the Exodus as if it was there that God created his nation. But I believe his real beginning was with me at the burning bush. We relive the Exodus every time we engage in worship, but it is the centrepiece rather than the first chapter of our story. The Lord began when he introduced himself to me, declaring his complete knowledge of Israel's suffering.

We had plunged into the depths of despair, convinced that we suffered alone; no one cared about us, we had no allies to save us, our cries were falling on deaf ears, and the god of our fathers lay buried in an impotent past.

When God met me at Horeb, he insisted that he was fully aware of our troubles. He was determined to lead us out of harsh slavery into the rich life of a new country. He had seen, he had heard, he was concerned and he would come down to us. He spelt this out in such detail that I wondered how stupid he thought I was: 'I have indeed seen the misery of my people in Egypt. I have heard them crying out because of their slave drivers, and I am concerned about their sufferings. So I have come down to rescue them from the hand of the Egyptians and to bring them up out of the land into a good and spacious land...and now the cry of the Israelites has reached me, and I have seen the way the Egyptians are oppressing them' (Ex 3:7–9).

My reaction was probably the same as yours would have been. If God was aware of us, why hadn't he acted earlier to rescue men, women and children who longed to be free? But he hadn't finished speaking, and he never took kindly to interruptions. I needed to listen longer, but I didn't like what I heard: 'So now go. I am sending you to Pharaoh to bring my people the Israelites out of Egypt' (Ex 3:10).

Egyptians around Pharaoh's palace who wished me well but cared nothing for the plight of Israel, had urged me to forget my Hebrew origins and enjoy the incredible stroke of luck which had secured my adoption into their affluent nation. Unwittingly they brought to a head the decision which would settle the matter once and for all. God was acting to deliver Israel and I was central to his plan. In saving us, he was mapping out a new future in which we would enter the fertile land of our dreams. It all sounded too good to be true. I knew the Israelites were already bitterly disillusioned. It would need more than a few grand promises to rouse their dying faith, but God was unfolding his purpose without telling us how he planned to fulfil it. As far as I was concerned, there was nothing on the near horizon to warrant optimistic acceptance of his will, but he screwed me hard to the floor: Was my faith practical? Would I risk obedience? Did I intend to push forward with no guarantee that he would vindicate me? Had I the nerve to trust him, even if he refused to reinforce his call with specific promises? In short, did I believe God?

Instinctively, I protested – and don't pretend that you would have smiled sweetly and obeyed in the same situation. I argued with God, squirming frantically to avoid the fate which closed around me like a net. Have you ever argued with God? Really argued? If not, you haven't made much progress to spiritual maturity because that involves constant grappling with God's way in your life, producing heated arguments, at least from your side. I've tried it many times and the lesson is sinking in – it doesn't work. Each time I argue, I shrink visibly, and my voice, high-pitched at first, fades into a feeble, apologetic murmur. I put up barriers, but they were hopelessly inadequate to protect me from the God who called me. One by one I lined up my objections; one by one he knocked them down.

Who am I?

Of course I know my name, I'm not that stupid, but I foresaw challenges from people who were suspicious of anyone claiming national authority. 'Who do you think you are?' would be the most likely objection, and I wanted to have God's answer ready. I'm not proud of my obstinacy, but I can't say I'm ashamed of it. It stood me in good stead all the time I led Israel, and I have learnt the hard way that impetuosity can be as awkward a liability as it is endearing an asset. At the time I had no friends there to offer me honest counsel, and my own judgements were based on the past in which I had achieved nothing to merit great confidence. I was not the man God needed.

You're probably thinking I was stubborn, but I was willing to be persuaded. Or was I? God, as always, was pointing me forward to rely on the rich promises which are part and parcel of his call. When he wants you to serve him, it's not your previous faith or your personal attributes which matter; it is his freedom to break into your life without explaining himself. He set me an awesome task, all the more daunting because of the price Pharaoh had put on my head. Egyptians who would easily recognise me were watching at the borders, and I would be lucky to enter the country unscathed, let alone confront Pharaoh in person.

I tried to question God, but he whacked me hard, and after all these years I can still feel it. My protest was simple enough: 'Who am I that I should go to Pharaoh and bring the Israelites out of Egypt?' (Ex 3:11). My intention was to manipulate a permanent escape from the call of God, and he rumbled me. I had plenty more barriers ready for the front line of defence if he smashed through this one because I was not yet willing to surrender to him. Typically, he didn't do what I expected; he ignored my question as though he hadn't heard a word.

If you denigrate yourself with a parade of humility which angles for sympathy and pleads for release from your obligation, you'll make no headway with the Lord. That is a lesson he taught me many times until he satisfied himself that I'd taken his point – which I did, a long time ago.

Who are you?

Some people were certain to grill me with questions, and I wanted answers for them. Surely my request was legitimate: I asked God to tell me his name and its meaning. We believe that the character of a person is expressed through his or her name. You may find it rather quaint when parents name their children after qualities like 'Faith' and 'Grace', or give them a name like 'Nathan', which acknowledges their son as God's gift. In our culture, as in many others, the name of a child is very important, and you are the poorer if you fail to take it seriously. We're not giving nice names to little children of whom we have fond hopes; we are prophesying significant qualities of character through the names we give them and we choose carefully, expecting God to guide us, even through those delightful family arguments which accompany the search for a baby's name.

God named himself to me as the God of our fathers: 'I am the God of your father, the God of Abraham, the God of Isaac and the God of Jacob' (Ex 3:6). That was both comforting and powerful because I clung to the assurance there and then that he understood our suffering. It was up to him to equip me to face a people whose allegiance I claimed in his new name. He turned me from the past to the future, and I searched for an appropriate name to indicate to the Israelites what the Lord would be to them.

My next question concealed a further objection. 'Suppose I go to the Israelites and say to them, "The God of your fathers has sent me to you," and they ask me, "What is his name?" Then what shall I tell them?' (Ex 3:13). Was that the question of a man understandably cautious or infuriatingly resistant to God?

In my view, the Lord answered me and he refused to answer. Tell me what you think of this for an ambiguous reply: 'I am who I am. This is what you are to say to the Israelites, "I AM has sent me to you"' (Ex 3:14). What sort of response was that? Would you be happy to address a nation with such a flimsy message from God? I doubt it, and neither was I. Our Hebrew language means that he could have been referring to the future, 'I will be who I will be.' I can well imagine the hotchpotch of unlikely sermons which preachers will dig out of a text like this one, and I'm glad I won't be around to hear them. The Lord was using a word-play to clarify the connection between his name and its meaning. The gist he intended, which took me a long time to work out, was that he would reveal his plans in future deeds and we should accept his assurance now without demanding a full explanation in advance. For the time being at least, we must switch the focus of our faith from the past to the future. One day we'll hold them together in an exciting tension, but not yet. My past exposed me as faltering and unreliable; my future promised a God who keeps his word against all contrary appearances. In other words, God was saying, 'Stop asking stupid questions, trust me and get on with it.' The conversation demonstrated that he was neither by-passing nor violating my human will, and I was not crushed; subdued, yes, but not crushed. Of course, my question was a red-herring – I'm not denying that. The Lord's reply linked his new name which I was to give Israel to the reality they already knew. This reassured me of his long-term purpose: 'I am who I am...This is what you are to say to the Israelites, "The Lord, the God of your fathers, the God of Abraham, the God of Isaac and the God of Jacob has sent me to you." This is my name for ever, the name by which I am to be remembered from generation to generation' (Ex 3:14–15).

You could not expect the Israelites to recognise their God in this new name. I could easily explain the purpose of my return to Egypt, but it was a bold and speculative initiative which attempted it in the name of a God called 'Yahweh', a name previously unused and unknown. All my confidence now lay in this name, an abbreviated form of his promise, by which God bound himself to keep his word to us. Here, the Lord offered to adopt Israel as his chosen people, while the Exodus established us as a coherent nation.

I announced a rescue I could not effect, to a people who could not achieve it, in the name of a God they did not recognise; and you wonder why I resisted my call! So I pushed forward another barrier, resisting the Lord with my next excuse.

This plan might not work

'What if they do not believe me or listen to me and say, "The Lord did not appear to you"?' (Ex 4:1). I anticipated cynical rejection from Israel and welcomed the possibility of another escape route from my call, but God responded with the assurance of a clear road ahead: 'I have promised to bring you up out of your misery in Egypt into the land of the Canaanites...the elders of Israel will listen to you...I know that the King of Egypt will not let you go unless a mighty hand compels him...after that he will let you go...and I will make the Egyptians favourably disposed towards this people...and so you will plunder the Egyptians' (Ex 3:17–21).

But I wanted more time. It's amazing how we hear God but take no notice of what he says. You may be itching to remind me that he answered my doubts when he promised that the elders would listen to me, but I sensed something which will prove as conspicuous a feature of Israel's attitude to her prophets as it has been of her attitude to me; unbelief, disobedience and rebellious complaint. The nation will cling to a prejudiced view of the past while the prophets plead for a right response in the present. The unbelief I foresee reflects my niggling uncertainty at the time God called me. It made me look for an immediate promise of his power which I wanted today; I was unwilling to wait until tomorrow.

God did meet me – incredibly, graciously, forcefully, and with a startling sign which he intended to be final. But I still hung back. I threw my rod on the ground when he instructed me, and it became a writhing snake which I grabbed by the tail. Then my hand was mysteriously afflicted with leprosy until I stabbed it into my coat for instant healing – and I didn't fall over. The powers he showed me were invitations promising strength for a specific job. 'Now go; I will help you speak and will teach you what to say' (Ex 4:12). But can you think of a worse nightmare for a man petrified of public speaking than to find himself forced to the centre of the platform he dreads, knowing that experienced speakers, ambitious for their own publicity, are jostling for the limelight he is desperate to avoid?

Please send someone else

I was down and nearly out, almost ready to concede, but I wasn't finished. In a final flailing attempt to stave off the call of God which was swamping my resistance, I produced the evasive classic of all time: 'O Lord, please send someone else to do it' (Ex 4:13). Its merit lay in its naked honesty, but otherwise it was shabby, and I'm ashamed of it now. This was neither a question nor an objection, it was not even a serious suggestion, it was my last resort. I was not playing for time, I was trying to run off the pitch; in fact, I was grabbing the whistle and blowing for the end of the game. If God was such a shrewd manager, why didn't he substitute me for someone who was eager to play?

My persistence won through in the end. Exasperated, the Lord lost patience and offered me a way out – a means of obedience, and also one that was face-saving. He spoke angrily, 'What about your brother, Aaron the Levite? I know he can speak well' (Ex 4:14). If only I had thought of Aaron before God did.

No doubt, you will remember my plea, 'O Lord, please send someone else to do it' – filing it away for your own future use. You've probably used it already. Some men volunteer other men in a blatant attempt to wriggle out of God's will. Some women retreat into catering, whether or not that is the contribution God wants from them. Some young people pursue personal ambi-

tions which are more concerned to capitalise on their own abilities than to trust God's provision for their lives. All claim that they are suffering from an infectious disease caught from me. But when God calls you, no one else will do; otherwise he would not have chosen you in the first place.

I am a proud man, foolishly proud, and I never said 'yes' to God. I deprived myself of the joy of explicit surrender as I moved into action with my request to Jethro for long-term leave from his sheep (Ex 4:18). I had agreed to obey God; I was doing what he wanted; there was no more resistance in me, and I served him with the best I could give. But there was never a moment when I looked him in the face and said, 'Yes, Lord.' I wish now that I could turn the clock back because I regret my loss, but it's my own fault. How often your own pride robs you long before it impoverishes anyone else.

I became a prophet, a leader, a commander, a judge, a shepherd of men, and anything else God asked of me. Above all, I accepted a unique, historical task. I was scared stiff many times, but I was also excited to follow a road whose sole guarantee was God's word: 'I am sending you to Pharaoh to bring my people the Israelites out of Egypt' (Ex 3:10). 'Go tell Pharaoh king of Egypt to let the Israelites go out of his country' (Ex 6:10). God turned the tables on Pharaoh, honouring all his promises to us, and the pressure he exerted eventually brought the Egyptians to their knees: 'Let's get away from the Israelites. The Lord is fighting for them against Egypt' (Ex 14:25).

When the Lord called me, I couldn't see the outcome, but he did. God expects us to serve him because he knows exactly what he will do, but we're usually slow to grasp that. We learn our lessons the hard way, but at least you can see how it has worked out in my life. Whatever you do, be sure to confirm my experience for yourself. It's hairy, but it's exciting, and I'd rather live than merely exist.

3

Let My People Go

If you pit an irresistible force against an immovable object, one of them must give way, and when I clashed with Pharaoh I made up my mind it wouldn't be me. Pharaoh fondly imagined that his only problem was an insignificant spokesman for his country's ragged bunch of Hebrew slaves whose name was Moses, but God stood against him. I came to him in the double strength of the Lord's assurances – 'I will be with you'; 'I will help you and teach you what to say' (Ex 3:12; 4:12) – with no intention of offering myself as a lamb for the slaughter. Aaron and I, with a vested interest in the outcome, delivered God's message to the Egyptian ruler: 'Let my people go, so that they may hold a festival to me in the desert' (Ex 5:1). We waited impatiently for Pharaoh's answer.

My encounters with Pharaoh were fascinating but gruelling. The calamities which struck Egypt weakened Pharaoh's resolve and paved the way for God to rescue us from slavery by leading us out of Egypt, through the sea and across the wilderness to the brink of the land he has promised us, Canaan. A succession of hilarious scenes delighted us as we watched the Egyptians progessively humiliated by God. But we also suffered agonising suspense as we fought for our freedom against a difficult Pharaoh who was deeply entrenched in a tyrant's determination to rule. I developed a grudging respect for this wily old monarch of Egypt who reluctantly returned the compliment. Neither of us conceded a willing inch, but one of us had to break. Pharaoh had always been a distant, cruel figure who cared nothing for the awful suffering he imposed on Israel, but in these meetings I found someone vaguely human. My regular audiences with him meant that we came to know each other well, each of us using every trick in the book to outwit the other. Fortunately for me, God was committed to a policy of sanctions against Egypt, and I was a willing accomplice when he imposed them.

We began with the see-saw neatly balanced, and both of us staked everything to bring it down at our own end. On the one hand, I demanded our freedom in God's name: 'Let my people go' (Ex 5:1). On the other hand, Pharaoh's reply was brief and to the point: 'Who is the Lord, that I should obey him and let Israel go? I do not know the Lord and I will not let Israel go' (Ex 5:2).

Aaron and I discussed our strategy, checked the balance of the see-saw, and withdrew to plan the next move. Meanwhile, Pharaoh proceeded with cynical calm. The same day, he issued a savage decree which made our captivity even worse. We had to maintain the existing quota of bricks, but now we must fetch our own straw. He struck hard at Israel, but he was really aiming at me because he knew that bitter captives would make me the scapegoat for their plight. Pharaoh was a shrewd man. As soon as we rejoined them, the mob did turn on us: 'May the Lord look upon you and judge you' (Ex 5:21). I lost the first round to Pharaoh, but I was soon ready for round two of a fight which had scarcely begun.

One day the prophets of Israel will confront the nation's rulers, arousing fierce controversy with their challenge. They will take personal risks to pursue their ministry, and many of them will pay the price for an outspoken obedience to God. My opposition to the Egyptian Pharaoh anticipated the way our prophets will announce God's will to an unruly nation. I wanted Pharaoh to let us go. A series of terrible disasters pressured, discouraged, appalled and eventually forced him to meet our demands, but the tedious struggle we endured showed me that you can't use the example of Pharaoh to argue that difficult circumstances produce submission to God. Circumstances may manipulate results, but they don't change hearts, and I pitched myself into an arduous tug-of-war with a stubborn oppressor.

The first plague turned the waters of the Nile into blood, and all the waters of Egypt followed suit (Ex 7:14–24). This eerie horror completely failed to impress Pharaoh, and I realised I had a tough opponent on my hands. He was more interested in the nuisance value of the plague than its serious difficulty. Frankly, he laughed at it, and his own magicians used their considerable occult powers to duplicate a messy inconvenience. I don't know how you cope with mockery when you're deadly serious, but it doesn't rate too highly with me. It either makes me mad, or it demoralises me.

Anyhow, the fish died and the water became unusable, but Pharaoh enjoyed the protection of privileged private supplies. He was totally committed to number one, with no concern for his subjects, and his nonchalant dismissal of the problem took the wind out of our sails. But I'm not sure other Egyptians felt so relaxed. A group of keen swimmers were bathing in the Nile when it all happened. You should have seen them when they waded out. It was even worse when they tried to find somewhere to wash it all off – is this what you call 'a bloodbath'? In my opinion, it won't be long before the Nile suffers permanent pollution without turning into blood, but we shall see.

Many ingredients of the later plagues were included in this opening skirmish: Pharaoh hardened his heart against us, he refused to yield to pressure and he turned down our plea for freedom. At the same time, God announced that his judgement was working through the blows which fell on Egypt: 'I will lay my hand on Egypt and with mighty acts of judgement I will bring out my divisions, my people the Israelites' (Ex 7:4). He made his intention clear: 'By this you will know that I am the Lord' (Ex 7:17), and this became the theme of the entire series. We understood what God was doing, but Pharaoh dismissed the problem. 'Pharaoh's heart became hard; he would not listen to Moses and Aaron, just as the Lord had said' (Ex 7:22).

Little did I realise that we had begun a long and gory series as Pharaoh enjoyed one week's respite before we moved from rivers of blood to frogs (Ex 7:25–8:15). We didn't know whether to laugh or cry, but there were frogs everywhere, and I mean everywhere. Swarming into the palace, frogs occupied every room. Pharaoh's wife climbed into bed and hit the ceiling when they croaked in her nightdress, while the entire palace enjoyed her screams. Hungry husbands, brow-beaten by vegetarian wives, rejoiced to find unlimited roast meat in dishes hot from the oven – frog-meat. All over the country, angry victims accused innocent jokers of one more tasteless prank. We found the whole thing so funny that we organised a competition, restricted to Hebrew slaves. We provided two sets of opening lines, and the entrants had to answer one of them: 'Waiter, waiter, there's a frog in my soup.' 'What did the Egyptian say to the frog?' Unfortunately, news of our irreverence leaked out, and Pharaoh took it badly, especially when he discovered that one of the palace slaves had swopped his favourite rice pudding for frog-spawn which he hadn't noticed until the first spoonful was in his mouth. Despite the royal anger, the jokes spawned faster than the frogs.

I hoped that two plagues would be enough to persuade Pharaoh to release us, but he was still fuming at us for poking fun at him. The frogs kept us in the realm of public nuisance rather than national disaster, and Pharaoh's wizards easily duplicated our effects, but they were not popular for multiplying the frogs. Thousands of street accidents pushed rescue services to the limit as people slithered into broken limbs on the spawn which lurked everywhere, and the children of Egypt revelled in the tadpoles. One day we'll invent a way of recording pictures but, alas, not yet. Meanwhile our artists, blessed with native Hebrew humour, produced some wonderful paintings of the plague of frogs, and we sheltered in our immunity from the Egyptian plight.

I approached Pharaoh, offering him the choice of time for the removal of the hazard and pressing its purpose upon him, 'so that you may know there is no-one like the Lord our God' (Ex 8:10). As soon as he had cleared the foul mess, he settled back, as people usually do, and his heart hardened (Ex 8:15). We took him to the water, but we couldn't make him drink.

We moved on to gnats (Ex 8:16–19). You should have seen them; remorseless clouds dropping from the sky to overwhelm Egypt. Within an hour, desperate victims had emptied shelves of insect spray from garden centres and snatched tubes of lotion from the chemists in a frantic rush for relief. We had given no notice of the plague, and we made no bid for freedom; the gnats were a surprise bonus for Pharaoh. He tried to dismiss this further difficulty as an unfortunate coincidence in the pile-up of trouble. We hoped to weaken his resolve to stay immovable by reinforcing ours to become irresistible. His officials were unable to copy this plague, and Pharaoh reluctantly conceded, 'This is the finger of God' (Ex 8:19). For what it's worth, I think his magicians were too scared of local anger to multiply the stinging insect hordes which covered Egypt, and they ceased to be a threat to us. Enough was enough, and they wanted no further blame for the mounting crisis caused by the plagues. The Egyptians were smothered in pimples, but

'Pharaoh's heart was hardened and he would not listen, just as the Lord had said' (Ex 8:19).

Insects were proving such a good idea for plagues that we stayed with them and moved on to flies: buzzing, filthy, elusive, persistent, disease-ridden flies (Ex 8:20–30). Flies are always a menace in hot climates, and our plague increased an existing scourge to epidemic proportions. The Egyptians loathed these prolific pests, and I returned confidently to Pharaoh who made no mention of the magicians we had sunk without trace. God introduced a distinction between Israel and Egypt which greatly comforted our people: 'But on that day I will deal differently with the land of Goshen, where my people live; no swarms of flies will be there' (Ex 8:22). We had been in Goshen since a previous Pharaoh allowed Joseph's family to settle there in the early years of acute famine (Gen 47:5–6).

The change in Pharaoh was barely noticeable, but it was there; the awkward ruler was beginning to weaken. He offered me a deal, and once the dealing starts the Hebrew will win. 'Go sacrifice to your God here in this land' was his first offer (Ex 8:25). My reply was polite as well as crafty: we couldn't dream of sacrificing to our God in Egypt, the Egyptians would not like it and we were too polite to insult their hospitality. In other words, 'No deal Pharaoh.' 'But this time also Pharaoh hardened his heart and would not let the people go' (Ex 8:32).

It was time to step up the pressure. We had caused a dreadful nuisance in Egypt, but now we would inflict serious damage. The next plague struck Egyptian livestock (Ex 9:1–7). Surely this would stop Pharaoh in his tracks. What more can God do to a people to turn them towards him? How low does anyone have to fall before he understands that God is calling him to his senses? Again, God put Hebrew minds at rest. 'The Lord will make a distinction between the livestock of Israel and that of Egypt, so that no animal belonging to the Israelites will die' (Ex 9:4). This created a terrible upset in

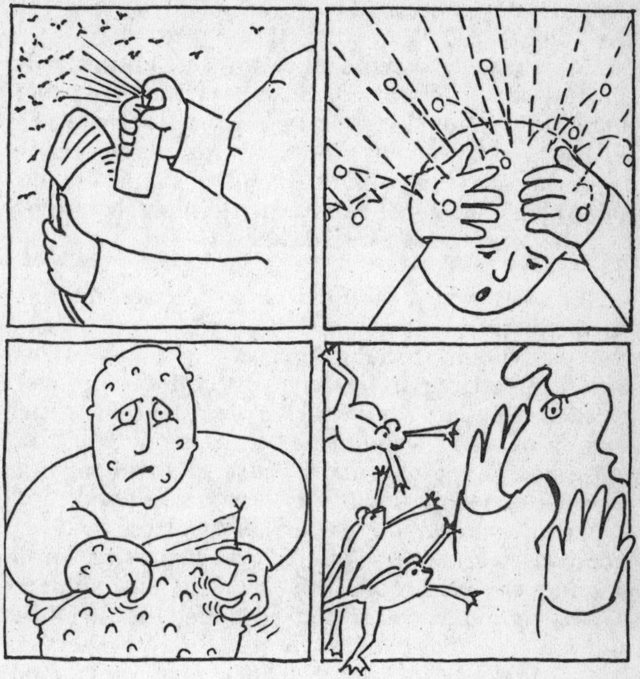

Egypt as devoted farmers lost beasts they had reared from birth, but the more we twisted Pharaoh's arm, the more he gritted his teeth and refused to budge: 'His heart was unyielding and he would not let the people go' (Ex 9:7).

Aaron usually did the dirty work in initiating the plagues while I supported him as a committed partner. This time God told us to reverse our usual roles. We did not introduce ourselves to the palace staff and we sought no audience with Pharaoh. We simply grabbed handfuls of filthy soot from a furnace, marched boldly into the palace, and I tossed the black dirt into the air (Ex 9:8–12).

Pharaoh watched us with detached amusement, until he started to itch. Revolting boils broke out all over his body, spreading through Egypt as the nation united with its monarch in extreme discomfort. Strangers pleaded together, 'You scratch my back and I'll scratch yours.' Men and beasts itched in harmony while our musicians composed suitable music to accompany the new craze, but the Egyptians were not amused. Boils appeared in the most embarrassing places, and you would often find yourself walking down the street or sitting in a crowded room with Egyptians who suddenly darted behind a tree or ducked under the furniture, and you knew they had disappeared for a quick scratch. No one said a word, but we all knew what was happening. It was great fun if you were an Israelite, but not otherwise. Egyptian magicians were determined to inflict similar suffering on us, but they couldn't stop scratching long enough to weave the necessary spells. 'But the Lord hardened Pharaoh's heart and he would not listen to Moses and Aaron' (Ex 9:12). We were still talking to a brick wall.

I became a careful student of the tactics of pressure and bluff. There are many ways of killing the cat. You can pressure one man into submission, but another stiffens and refuses to yield. You can cajole one man into agreement; but another digs in his heels and won't move. You can provoke one man to accept a challenge, but another smells a rat and refuses to fight. One man knows when he is losing an argument and withdraws quietly, but another presses on to the bitter end, however badly he is beaten. Now I was testing Pharaoh and he was testing me; what sort of men were in opposition on behalf of Egypt and Israel? Pharaoh was a tough leader, but so was I, and we clashed head-on.

You may think you've been caught in a few downpours, but you never saw the hail which fell on Egypt as the seventh plague (Ex 9:13–35). It wasn't a bad storm, it was a torrential disaster. It pelted down, but only on Egypt; an act of God rather than a freak in the weather. The Egyptians listened in vain for reports of violent storms elsewhere and lamented their inadequate insurance. Huge hailstones ruined healthy crops and ruthlessly exposed building deficiencies. With the whole country reeling from heaven's outburst, it seemed a good time to intensify the pressure on Pharaoh. I repeated the purpose behind this protracted agony. 'This is what the Lord, the God of the Hebrews, says: "Let my people go, so that they may worship me, or this time I will send the full force of my plague against you and against your officials and your people, so that you may know that there is no-one like me in all the earth...I have raised you up for this very purpose, so that I might show you my power and that my name might be proclaimed in all the earth"' (Ex 9:13–16).

I sensed, rightly, that we were into a long season of tough bargaining, but Egypt was coming apart at the seams. It was nothing I could prove, but there was an unmistakable scent in the air, the scent of victory, although it was still a long way off. We gave Pharaoh warning of the hail, urging him to protect his livestock. Those of his staff who feared the word of the Lord listened to us and led their animals inside for shelter (Ex 9:20). Others were scornful and did nothing (Ex 9:21).

Take note that when God acts in power, he doesn't convince everyone; some stand in awe while others openly disregard the evidence, suffering the consequences of their deliberate contempt.

Once again, God separated Israel from Egypt: 'The only place it did not hail was the land of Goshen, where the Israelites were' (Ex 9:26). We had day-trippers galore in Goshen as Egyptian families piled in for a brief respite from their own downpour. Our people shook their heads, wringing their hands in obvious regret that they were not free to capitalise on the commercial possibilities of these mass excursions. I rebuked Pharaoh for his hard heart, letting him know that his show of repentance didn't fool me. He had confessed his sin, 'This time I have sinned, the Lord is in the right, and I and my people are in the wrong' (Ex 9:27), but I knew this was no more than a way of saying, 'Please Moses, get this storm off my back.' I told Pharaoh that I'd seen through him: 'I know that you and your officials still do not fear the Lord God' (Ex 9:30). But you can't force hasty concessions from long-in-the-tooth leaders, and Pharaoh soon confirmed my suspicions that he was not serious about constructive talks: 'When Pharaoh saw that the rain and hail and thunder had stopped, he sinned again: he and his officials hardened their hearts' (Ex 9:34).

The whole affair was turning into a farce. How long must these gruesome plagues go on? But this was no time to relent or withdraw; we had to drive home our advantage, not change our tactics. If we squeezed Pharaoh hard enough, we'd choke him in the end.

What about a plague of locusts (Ex 10:1–20)? The world has not seen the last of these insect monsters. Their insatiable appetites and frenzied breeding are already legendary, and they will return regularly to terrify helpless farmers who struggle in hot climates. Aaron and I pleaded with Pharaoh but he, typically, hardened his heart against us, paving the way for God to demonstrate his power through the locusts. Many Egyptians were losing heart, and their sinking morale sapped any remaining allegiance to a stubborn ruler. 'Pharaoh's officials said to him, "How long will this man be a snare to us? Let the people go, so that they may worship the Lord their God. Do you realise that Egypt is ruined?"' (Ex 10:7). We were twisting Pharaoh's arm, but he still wanted to strike a hard bargain with a tempting offer: a few of us could go, but not all of us. I rejected the deal, calling his bluff and digging in for the push to complete victory.

God told me to stretch out my staff over Egypt (Ex 10:12). 'By morning the wind had brought the locusts; they invaded all Egypt' (Ex 10:13–14). The marauding insects left nothing untouched. They covered the entire land with a black blanket of destruction, greedily devouring all remaining vegetation and provoking the histrionics of females whose usual nightmares were caused by nothing more awesome than spiders. 'Nothing green remained on tree or plant in all the land of Egypt' (Ex 10:15). Pharaoh quickly offered more of his transparent repentance. 'I have sinned against the Lord your God and against you. Now forgive my sin once more and pray to the Lord your God to take this deadly plague away from me' (Ex 10:16–17). I thought our negotiations were too delicate for me to refuse him, but again he didn't take long to confirm my suspicions about his sincerity. 'The Lord hardened Pharaoh's heart, and he would not let the Israelites go' (Ex 10:20).

In some ways the darkness of the ninth plague was an anti-climax, but the tables were turning (Ex 10:21–29). I gave Pharaoh no warning and made no plea for freedom, but he summoned me with a fresh offer, like management grappling with an intransigent union: 'Go, worship the Lord. Even your women and children may go with you; only leave your flocks and herds behind' (Ex 10:24). He hoped I would settle for a bird in the hand, but I went for two in the bush. This was a concession, and I seized the initiative, grabbed Pharaoh by the throat and snatched the upper hand he let slip. He weakened, and I surrendered nothing. 'Our livestock too must go with us; not a hoof is to be left behind. We have to use some of them in worshipping the Lord our God' (Ex 10:26). As if I would fall for his ploy by agreeing to leave a massive deposit to guarantee our return. Did he really think I was that daft, even after nine plagues?

Pharaoh's assumption that I would even dream of accepting his terms stung me, and I responded by tightening the screw for all our demands. You may not think a plague of darkness is too bad, but try coping day and night with total blackness. Not even a candle is possible because you can't find the right drawer. People stumbled, collided, crashed and fell, breaking bones they scarcely knew they had. Accidents reached those parts which other plagues hadn't touched, while rampant looting and unscrupulous burglary hurried Egypt towards anarchy. Eager young men bumped into eligible young ladies, and regretted their good fortune when the light returned to expose the appearance of their blind dates. Eight plagues had frayed the national temper which was snapping at the ninth, and all Egypt lived on a short fuse. In the hardness of his heart, Pharaoh lost his temper and threw us out of the palace, a fatal move. Every fighter knows that if you keep your cool you will beat the man who loses his. 'But the Lord hardened Pharaoh's heart, and he was not willing to let the people go. Pharaoh said to Moses, "Get out of my sight. Make sure that you do not appear before me again. The day you see my face you will die" (Ex 10:28). The thought that I might never see Pharaoh again was music to my ears, but we fumbled in the dark when we tried to find the exit.

The final plague was awful, but it sustained the difference between us and our oppressive masters. God destroyed the firstborn of all living things in Egypt (Ex

11:1–10). Pharaoh received a graphic warning, and he knew our threats were not idle. When I brought God's announcement to him, I was explicit about the scale of the approaching doom: 'About midnight I will go through Egypt. Every firstborn son in Egypt will die, from the firstborn son of Pharaoh...to the firstborn son of the slave girl...and all the firstborn of the cattle as well' (Ex 11:4–5). This time Pharaoh's privileged position could not shield him from appalling tragedy. I was determined to let Egypt know how callously he had dismissed our repeated pleas for freedom from slavery. His indifference to us, and his selfish disregard for his own people, got under my skin and up my nose and I snapped. White with anger, I left Pharaoh; in fact, I stormed out (Ex 11:8).

Can you imagine what it was like when this plague struck Egypt? The news broke with a wail here and a cry there, but it gathered force in a fearful crescendo which soon became the deafening noise of outraged sorrow. Every culture I know puts an incredibly high price on its firstborn. They are the pride and joy of the family, and parents never recover from their premature loss. It took only one strike to wipe out the firstborn of Egypt. We had laughed our way through the previous disasters, but now we were quiet. This was the final blow; nothing worse could hit Egypt as some tormented families raged in anger while others collapsed in the numbing grief of bereavement. We wanted to celebrate our new feast of Passover, but we feared to gloat.

Egypt was ready to throw in the towel. Many people remembered me well from my early days, or knew of me by reputation and were happy for our release. They argued with their Pharaoh, forcing him to see that he must not go on, least of all without their support. A few foreign slaves were not worth the fuss, whatever the cost to the king's pride. The drama of the plagues highlighted God's determination to save Israel and establish us as an independent nation with its own land.

These events are already central to our national traditions, our worship and our education. The Passover tradition sees to it that we will never forget the Exodus. It is central to our worship. While our children are young, we teach them what it means to be Hebrew. God's instructions were clear: 'And when your children ask you, "What does this ceremony mean to you?" then tell them, "It is the Passover sacrifice to the Lord, who passed over the Israelites in Egypt and spared our homes when he struck down the Egyptians"' (Ex 12:26–27). 'You may tell your children and grandchildren how I dealt harshly with the Egyptians and how I performed my signs among them, and that you may know that I am the Lord' (Ex 10:2).

Before he unleashed the final plague on Egypt, God gave us detailed instructions. On the tenth day of the year, each Israelite family had to take a lamb which could be shared if families were small. In fact, it could be a lamb or a kid, but it must be a young male in prime condition. We were to keep the animal for four days before slaughtering it in the early evening. The same night we had to prepare the meal – roasted meat, bitter herbs and unleavened bread. We must eat quickly (not that some of us needed telling), with our cloaks tucked into our belts and our sandals on our feet. Presumably, this was to be ready for a quick getaway if it became possible. God told us to take the blood of the slaughtered lamb or kid and daub it round the edges of our door frames. When he came to destroy the firstborn of Egypt, he would see the blood and pass over our houses. It all seemed a bit strange, but it's more important to obey God than quibble about the way he works. His promise was more than welcome. 'No destructive plague will touch you when I strike Egypt' (Ex 12:13). The blood kept us safe, and we followed every instruction with meticulous care; there were no more jokes for the time being. We may suffer badly in years to come, but we shall neglect the Passover or the privilege of being Hebrew at our peril (see 2 Kings 23:21-23).

As soon as Pharaoh heard of the mass slaughter in Egypt, he knew he was beaten. The loss in his own house broke his heart, and at last the suffering of his people reached him. During the night he summoned me with an urgent plea. 'Up! Leave my people, you and the Israelites. Go, worship the Lord as you requested. Take your flocks and herds, as you have said, and go' (Ex 12:31-32).

These bizarre plagues did their job; they softened up Pharaoh and convinced him that further defiance was a pointless form of national suicide. In his final rebellion, when he changed his mind and chased us, his hostility proved fatal as well as futile. The irresistible force was shifting the immovable object, but it was still too early to count our chickens – they weren't hatched yet. I'll finish the story of Pharaoh's downfall in the next chapter. Meanwhile, we didn't need telling twice to leave Egypt.

4
The Way Out – Exodus

We were a bunch of runaway slaves when we left Egypt but a new nation when we walked out of the Red Sea. God's amazing power achieved a dramatic change in our national fortune and revealed his lasting purpose for Israel – a purpose which will unfold over the centuries. You'll waste your time if you search Egyptian records to check our story because no Pharaoh in his right mind celebrates the annihilation which our escape inflicted on Egypt. This Pharaoh had every intention of dismissing us as trivial fugitives who had cheated their way out of his unmerciful clutches. There was no way he would write us into his country's record of honour. Egypt lost a welcome source of cheap labour as well as its complete army when we left, but that was not the total overthrow of the country. I'm afraid you'll have to accept Israelite records and take my word for the details.

It must be obvious to you that our rescue was vital to us. Israel will always regard it as unique and wonderful, but it won't even ruffle the surface of Egyptian history. We describe our captivity in Egypt, our escape from slavery and our entry to a new future across the marshy waters of the Red Sea, known more accurately as the 'Reed Sea'. This Exodus is the salvation event of our faith, providing both its historical basis and its unceasing inspiration. You can expect future prophets to hark back to Israel's early days, not in empty nostalgia but in wistful regret and angry denunciation of the sins of their own day. The Exodus tradition will maintain a permanent influence on the future of our religion; its life, its message and its worship. I do not intend to catalogue each incident in detail, rather to highlight the main features of the story with alliterative headings. You will find them easy to repeat if you have your own teeth, but otherwise, please be careful. They could end up the other side of the room, and I don't want you to sue me for damages or dentures.

Faltering

The Exodus exposes the weakness, the hesitation and the anxiety of Israel. We faltered, despite God's specific commitment to save us. We had thought of nothing else but leaving Egypt – 'The Israelites groaned in their slavery and cried out' (Ex 2:28) – and we could scarcely take it in that at last freedom was ours for the taking. The Lord wore down Pharaoh's resistance through the devastating plagues – rivers of blood, frogs, gnats, flies, the loss of livestock, boils, hail, locusts, darkness and the death of all firstborn sons. The Egyptian ruler melted slowly, until his final agreement to let us leave the country we hated. Can you imagine the excitement which swept through the camp and motivated our frenzied preparations? But as soon as we realised Pharaoh's army was chasing us, we buckled at the knees and our confidence collapsed. The people lost their nerve and rounded furiously on me (Ex 14:11–12).

We didn't march, we trudged as if we had lead in our boots. God was telling us to move forward, but we could only look backwards. He wanted us to fix our eyes on him, but they were glued to the pursuing enemy. 'As Pharaoh approached, the Israelites looked up, and there were the Egyptians, marching after them. They were terrified and cried out to the Lord' (Ex 14:10).

If you were planning our exit from Egypt, you could have done all sorts of things to make thorough preparations. You might have publicised a conference to discuss the pros and cons of the journey so that you could assess the level of support for your leadership. You could have weighed the likely problems of food and water against the meagre rations you had in Egypt. You could have set the risk of Pharaoh changing his mind against the chances of putting a good distance between you before he could do that. You could have argued the possibility of women and children failing to cope with the harsh conditions of travelling against their alternative fate if they stayed in Egypt. But we didn't arrange a conference, and rightly so.

We left Egypt as soon as Pharaoh nodded his head and told us to go. 'On that very day the Lord brought the Israelites out of Egypt by their divisions' (Ex 12:51). You don't leave the Exodus till tomorrow if you can have it today. We paused just long enough to take Egyptian valuables with us to hasten our escape from the slavery we hated into the freedom for which we had dreamed day and night, but none of us had ever known (Ex 12:35–36). We had to be firm. Thrifty but impractical women were packing everything they could hide away, hoping we wouldn't notice the kitchen sink. Grannies had grown attached to knick-knacks they refused to abandon in Egypt. Dads found they had more sentiment than sense as we caught scores of them stuffing forbidden extras into places they thought no one would find them, while we launched a life-and-death bid for safety. I honestly believe some of them would have cheerfully hired Egyptian removal chariots if they thought there was discount for bulk bookings. Eventually, we were ready. It seemed to take ages, but really it was very quick, with no more accidents in packing than a few ruffled feathers.

God was giving us a new beginning with God through the rescue he called me to lead, and I announced it publicly to Israel. Once you take the decision to move, you don't hang around for second thoughts, and you don't waver when you hit snags. But we did. We lost sight of our goal, and our difficulties piled up; we fell at the first fence when we marched out of Egypt.

Fear

'The Israelites looked up, and there were the Egyptians marching after them. They were terrified and cried out to the Lord' (Ex 14:10). God had promised our freedom, vindicating himself by forcing Pharaoh to agree to our repeated demands to leave Egypt. We should have pressed on; we should have learned by now that God would handle Pharaoh; we should have treated today's catastrophe as tomorrow's non-event, which it usually is. But we didn't. A craven fear paralysed us as we rushed from the euphoria of our exit to the recriminations of which I was the principal target. The nation vented its frustration by hurling accusations at me which they disguised as questions. I know it was not so much personal anger as bitter disappointment directed at the leader they held responsible for their dilemma, and I know the buck stops with me, but it still hurt. Yes, I've heard it before, a leader who wants the credit for success must take the blame for failure, but I found too many brickbats and too few credits.

People have many ways of showing their fear, and I saw most of them on our march from Egypt. We were scared of Pharaoh's army when he chased us to seize back valuable slaves, and we panicked as chaos broke out among a people demoralised by their own helplessness; in fact we stopped thinking. Israel rounded on

Aaron and me, although our track record was one of reliable service. The long-term perspective was drowning in short-term despair, dragging the purpose of God with it. 'Was it because there were no graves in Egypt that you brought us to the desert to die?' the people raged. 'What have you done by bringing us out of Egypt? Didn't we say to you in Egypt, "Leave us alone; let us serve the Egyptians"? It would have been better for us to serve the Egyptians than to die in the desert' (Ex 14:12).

If only one Hebrew had said to me, 'Come on Moses, God has a way out of this. He hasn't brought us this far to abandon us. Let's find out what he wants us to do.' That would have given me a great opportunity to stir Israel to bold faith, but no one put the right question and I couldn't give the right answer. We are bound to ask questions when we suffer, but let's make them positive so that they can lead us forward. Israel put the wrong questions, and they led us into a futile cul-de-sac.

Pharaoh

As far as I was concerned, we'd seen the last of Pharaoh when ten plagues persuaded him to let us leave Egypt, but he had other ideas. It's true that God was always one step ahead of this persistent tyrant, although you'd never have thought so from our behaviour, but Pharaoh harassed us out of active trust in the Lord and into terror; never as difficult an achievement as it should have been. He soon regretted the loss of his slaves, and when Pharaoh regretted anything, he moved fast. 'When the king of Egypt was told that the people had fled, Pharaoh and his officials changed their minds about them and said, "What have we done? We have let the Israelites go and have lost their services"' (Ex 14:5). He rehardened his heart, as if the thing wasn't granite already, mustered his eager forces and set out to recapture us. 'He had his chariot made ready and took his army with him.

THE WAY OUT – EXODUS

He took six hundred of the best chariots, along with all the other chariots of Egypt, with officers over all of them. The Lord hardened the heart of Pharaoh king of Egypt, so that he pursued the Israelites' (Ex 14:6–8).

We hit rock bottom as soon as we realised the chase was on, and I realised that the entire camp had forgotten how God had spoken to us and acted powerfully among us. We were scared to move into the path of dry land when the waters parted before us, but Pharaoh never flinched in his pursuit. He was hunting us down and nothing would deter him. We were following God, and we were easily deterred. Does that ring any bells with you? Don't you find that your opponents are often more committed than you are? Any fear Pharaoh had of the sea was less than his fear of losing slaves. 'The Israelites went right through the sea on dry ground, with a wall of water on their right and on their left. The Egyptians pursued them, and all Pharaoh's horses and chariots and horsemen followed them into the sea' (Ex 14:22–24).

The whole story is one of frenzy, panic, uncontrolled noise, petrified silence, and a complete breakdown of discipline, but also one of the wonderful intervention of God. Once he played his hand to save us, he destroyed Pharaoh's stomach for further resistance. Egypt wanted us for slaves, but God had chosen us to be his nation living in freedom, and you can't thwart God when he's made up his mind. 'In the morning watch the Lord looked down from the pillar of fire and cloud at the Egyptian army and threw it into confusion...he made the wheels of their chariots come off so that they had difficulty driving. And the Egyptians said, "Let's get away from the Israelites. The Lord is fighting for them against Egypt"' (Ex 14:24–25). The Lord trusted me with his power, and I acted in prompt obedience. I did what he told me to do: '"Stretch out your hand over the sea..." and at daybreak the sea went back to its place. The Egyptians were fleeing towards it, and the Lord swept them into the sea... Not one of them survived' (Ex 14:26–28).

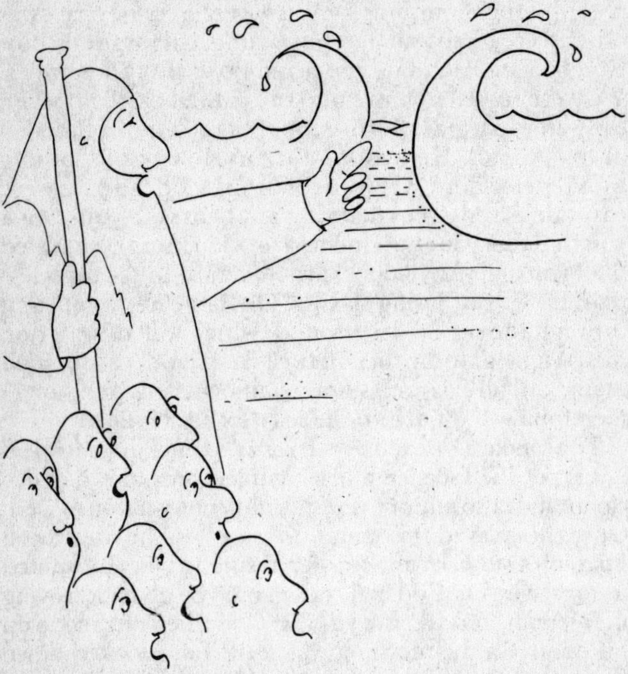

When the waters first parted, we stood there, staring at something none of us understood. It doesn't happen every day, and that's all there is to it; the opening of the sea did not fit with our world view. It must have amused God to make a nonsense of our scepticism, and we had to move quickly. Later, when the Egyptians drowned in front of us, we made a deafening noise. We acted like old hands at miracles, with short memories of our recent disgrace. Everyone cheered and shouted, hoisting me onto their shoulders in an impromptu victory parade, while I tried in vain to forget the furious onslaught of their complaints which were still loud in my ears. And that was the end of Pharaoh.

Faith

We experienced a miracle in the Exodus. The Lord linked a supernatural demonstration to an ordinary event. We did not achieve our salvation by our own means, yet we had to play a part by showing practical trust, which is the way salvation works.

When we left Egypt, I knew God was speaking to me about our immediate route. I felt distinctly uncomfortable about taking the most direct road, and I was learning to pay close attention to such niggles. I prayed simply, assuring God that I would take the path he chose – if I knew what it was. And that's where we often find ourselves when we're seeking guidance. I was anxious to consult him about the most basic decisions because it's much easier to find God's will if you have already prayed for him to show you what it is. It at least means that you're looking for signs which indicate guidance.

We could have travelled straight through Philistine country, but hostile natives would probably have frightened us into a hasty retreat. God knew that in advance, and led us by a roundabout route into the desert. 'For God said, "If they face war, they might change their minds and return to Egypt." So God led the people around by the desert road towards the Red Sea' (Ex 13:17–18). As if the people of Israel could ever change their minds! How could anyone be cynical enough even to hint at the possibility? 'By day the Lord went ahead of them in a pillar of cloud to guide them on their way and by night in a pillar of fire to give them light, so that they could travel by day or night' (Ex 13:21).

We were constantly amazed how the daytime cloud and the night-time fire remained in front of us, always in sight and always sensitive to our pace. Cloud and fire were the evidence I needed to justify our strange route to a people who had argued strongly for the quickest road away from Egypt, and we began our journey with enthusiasm and high morale. If God does settle on the unexpected way for you, you can be sure he will make his reason clear at some point, but it may not be as soon as you want. You are only obedient to him if you go his way, irrespective of criticism or consequences. The route we took could not have been predicted, and it ran counter to popular thinking, but God went ahead, calling me to keep my nerve before a critical people. His summons on my life; my return to Egypt to lead the people out in his new name, Yahweh; my confident assurances that he would bring us to safety, and the lengthy series of plagues on Egypt fed into the Exodus to demonstrate God's ability to direct his chosen nation by leading us to the land where we could serve him in freedom.

So we trusted God's word. Perhaps I'm using the word 'we' rather generously, because the people struggled to trust anything except the invincibility of the Egyptians. At the first sight of Pharaoh's chasing hordes, we were terrified. You may think that's understandable, since our enemies were a well-equipped army and we were defenceless runaways, but you can't go on excusing unbelief for ever. I was now sold out to God. I had burned my boats behind me, ready to stake everything on him who had not led us so far to bless us with pleasant experiences or to make fools of us. That's not his style; he does not play around with us, he builds our faith through hard lessons. We often miss what he is teaching us because we grab at premature blessing without searching long enough for his longer-term purpose.

When Israel turned on me with their angry complaints, I was ready for them, prepared by a gracious work of God in my own life. 'Do not be afraid. Stand firm and you will see the deliverance the Lord will bring you today. The Egyptians you see today you will never see again. The Lord will fight for you; you only need to be still' (Ex 14:13–14). Pharaoh threatened me with death if I saw his face again (Ex 10:28), but God's promise greatly comforted me. I expect all sorts of people will lift my words from their original context to draw personal strength, but I hope the Exodus circumstances will be a lasting example of the way God works. 'Do not be afraid. Stand firm and you will see the deliverance the Lord will bring you today.'

I announced God's word to Israel. Obedient to his prompting, I stretched out my staff over the sea and the waters parted before us. I would have looked a fool if nothing had happened. The staff, which spells safety for the sheep and danger for the predator, might have proved powerless over the water, but that is the risk you take when you go out on a limb for God. His promise was clear enough – 'The Egyptians will know that I am the Lord when I gain glory through Pharaoh, his chariots and his horsemen' (Ex 14:18), and his summons was simple enough – 'Tell the Israelites to move on' (Ex 14:15). Now we had to see how it all worked.

I had urged Israel to stand still (Ex 14:13–14), and God was saying 'move on' (Ex 14:15). That is not as contradictory as it sounds, because the best way of standing firm in the face of opposition is to press ahead. That may be a paradox, but it's certainly not a contradiction; attack is the best form of defence. Suddenly, the pillar of cloud moved from the front of Israel to the rear, separating us from the Egyptians. God had moved between us and our enemies in a decisive act of protective love. In the moment of our decision – to move forward or to be rooted to the spot – we lost sight of the enemy and trusted God. He divided the waters before us, and the sea-bed became dry land. As a tool in the hand of God, the raging wind became an ally of Israel.

Forward march

There is some uncertainty about the precise sequence of events, but don't let that surprise you. Our methods of recording history are far from sophisticated because we rely on personal memories and impressions, and our accounts reflect that variety. Let's face it, the whole event was unusual. How many times has the sea split open for you? If it did, would you risk an afternoon stroll, grateful that you'd saved the fare for the ferry?

Pharaoh's army terrified us with its chase, and we faltered badly. God called me to raise my staff over the waters in a supreme act of spiritual courage. On the same night a hurricane divided the waters which allowed us to cross over but drowned the pursuing Egyptians. Those are the essential facts of a marvellous story, gleaned from many memories.

When people panic, when the enemy presses you hard, and when you as leader suffer criticism, you may wonder what to do next, but it's typical of God to say, 'Move on' (Ex 14:15). Setbacks don't pressurise him into abandoning his plans. He can alter the form of his guidance whenever he chooses, and he keeps us on our toes for new directions. The pillar of cloud and fire drove us from the rear instead of leading us from the front, which would have caused hopeless confusion unless I had persuaded Israel to offer today's obedience and not assume yesterday's was still valid. If we had insisted on keeping the cloud and fire in front of us, on the grounds that that was God's tried and tested guidance, we would have gone round and round in circles. God could have enjoyed a good laugh at our expense, but otherwise it would be pointless folly in the midst of serious business. Someone had to stay in touch with the Lord to know when he was saying 'today' and to act on it.

I'd love to tell you how we strode forward confidently in perfect discipline, singing the songs of Israel in spontaneous harmony, but we didn't. We were a disorderly mob panicking our way to freedom. Yet we did go forward, and in obeying God's word, 'move on', we walked into a unique miracle. How many more miracles await those who move on, but are lost to those who don't?

Future

The purpose of the Exodus was as much for our future as our rescue. We crossed the sea and pressed on with the minimum of delay. As soon as we had learned a new hymn to celebrate the Exodus, we resumed our journey from the Red Sea into the desert of Shur (Ex 15:1,22). The climax of the hymn gave our confidence a terrific boost, but I'll tell you more about that when I talk about our worship. We sang it with unprecedented gusto. 'The Lord will reign for ever and ever' (Ex 15:18) – an original version of 'Our God Reigns'. In those early days of heady triumph, we were ready for anything, except hardship. We praised God, enjoying our experience of his power. That single deliverance will inspire Israel for hundreds of years, probably for all time, but it will also tempt us to wallow in past glories. These great events must lead us into a stronger future, not complacency and lethargy. 'In your unfailing love you will lead the people you have redeemed. In your strength you will guide them to your holy dwelling' (Ex 15:13).

Our song hurried us forward, and the ladies led our worship. 'Then Miriam the prophetess, Aaron's sister, took a tambourine in her hand, and all the women followed her, with tambourines and dancing. Miriam sang to them...' (Ex 15:20–21). As with our hymns, I'll discuss this later, but meanwhile, don't start moaning and grumbling, please. Our dancers come in all shapes and sizes, as yours do. They weren't all built for attractive movement, as you are only too quick to point out, but they were just as excited by the Exodus as those who were more suitably designed, and we loved them enough to let them express their joy. Perhaps you live at a time when understanding love is in short supply, in which case dancing in worship might prove controversial among you. We accepted it happily, sharing the enthusiasm of those who danced or rattled tambourines. You'll be a much happier person if you do the same. People who felt the wonder of their own safety had few problems with exuberant women, while the few who felt nothing objected to the extravagance, calling it 'irreverent'.

In response to the Exodus, Israel turned to God and offered me her unconditional loyalty: 'The people feared the Lord and put their trust in him and in Moses his servant' (Ex 14:31). I'm ashamed to admit that this moving pledge lasted about five minutes, as long as it took us to hit our first snag – lack of water in the wilderness of Shur. But what else can you expect in a desert? 'So the people grumbled against Moses' (Ex 15:24).

In the Exodus, God confirmed that we were his chosen people. He established his claim on our allegiance as well as our gratitude, so that our knowledge of him is rooted in historical fact. We discovered that he has a purpose for us which he expresses with compassionate power. We recognised his ability to act mightily, and this produced our faith in him as the living God. When we walked safely on the sea-bed we knew he was forming a nation for whom the Exodus would be the focal point of worship. He gave us a way out when there was none, and he created living hope out of total despair. Pharaoh hemmed us in, but God gave us space. Now he was calling us to remember these things and to move on. It has been my privilege, and often my terrible burden, to lead Israel by announcing, experiencing, explaining and celebrating this Exodus. I am not seeking a special place in our history, but I suspect that is what I have won.

5
My Father-in-Law

You probably know the saying: 'Behind every successful man lurks a surprised mother-in-law.' It's a good joke because it pulls the leg of the proverbial battle-axe and I'm all in favour of anything which does that. But it isn't true. It is much nearer the mark, although not nearly so funny, to say, 'Behind every successful man stands a surprised father-in-law.'

The relationship between a man and his father-in-law is strangely unexplored, and I shall plug the gap by reflecting on my friendship with Jethro, Zipporah's father, who had the dubious privilege of being my father-in-law. Initially, he was wary of me, but we soon grew to trust each other deeply, which greatly strengthened both of us.

A man's mother-in-law seldom causes him too many problems. All the jokes about this relationship prove that a healthy marriage involves plenty of light-hearted fun between the two of them. Of course, you can expect bitter recriminations if the marriage breaks down, but that's another matter. Few mums threaten their own daughters, and the two women happily share a conspiracy to tame one man. The son-in-law treats his wife's mother with cheeky affection, and she only dominates him if he's so weak that he deserves to suffer the tyranny of petticoat rule.

By contrast, a girl faces an uphill struggle with her husband's mother, and there are not too many jokes around to smooth their path. Mother-in-law hates releasing her son to the uncertain care of a girl she regards with jealous disapproval. She has doted on him from his cradle, pandering to his selfish whims, while he has carefully trained her to accept his peculiar taste in food and clothes and to tolerate his objectionable personal habits. Neither of them really wants another woman marching in to demand her full marital rights from a new husband. Men joke about mother-in-law, but women don't; too few of them think it's a laughing matter.

Now, you needn't start spluttering, especially if you have a daughter-in-law; just read what I'm saying, and remember, I may have consulted your daughter-in-law before I wrote it.

All right, I am exaggerating. Things do improve, love and understanding do develop, but you're not seriously suggesting that there's nothing in what I'm saying, are you? These distressing difficulties will continue until our Hebrew view of marriage becomes standard practice: 'For this reason a man will leave his father and mother and be united to his wife, and they will become one flesh' (Gen 2:24). How often parents at a wedding presume to offer son or daughter-in-law a welcome into their family, when the truth is that the young couple cannot be welcomed anywhere; they are leaving both families to start one of their own, not because they are expecting a baby but because they are married. Only a son can make his mum and dad see this; it's disastrous if his young wife tries to put her foot down, but too often the complacent male is content to allow his wife and mother to jostle over him — although, frankly, he's not worth the bother. He expects the women in his life to dote on him so much that they jump happily every time he snaps his fingers. That's fine as a husband if you can get away with it, but it's a bit rough on an unsuspecting bride. If you are a mother-in-law yourself, try to remember how it was for you, and leave your daughter-in-law a better legacy.

All that should have been familiar ground, but I have also considered my relationship with my father-in-law, Jethro. In our pre-occupation with female tensions we have failed to examine this important aspect of family life.

The relationship between father-in-law and son-in-law begins with mutual suspicion. An unknown young man taking an active interest in an attractive young woman, arouses her father's protective interest. He takes anxious note of the young man's appearance, scrutinising him for any trace of youthful decadence or moral depravity. He is watching someone who wants nothing more than to pay him the supreme compliment of falling in love with his daughter, but that's not the view of a guarded dad. Now there are two cocks in one nest; the older who deludes himself that he is still young enough, and the younger who is sure that he's a fount of adult wisdom. Dad melts warily as his wife chides him into the hesitant conclusion, 'She could do a lot worse;' both of them too smug to realise that the young man also has parents who don't believe any girl will make their son happy in the manner to which they have foolishly accustomed him.

The prospective father-in-law edges reluctantly towards a grudging acceptance of the inevitable, taking a route which passes through his daughter's wedding. I have attended hundreds of weddings as leader of Israel. The most embarrassing moment is always the speech which the bride's father inflicts on the unfortunate guests, and I can understand why some of them drink enough to soften the agony. (Please don't write to me, I'm not condoning drunkenness; I just hate that part of a wedding.) The guests cringe, the bride shrinks, and her mother 'dies' as she listens to an accomplished husband reducing himself to a drooling idiot who expects the captive audience to agree that his daughter is perfect, beautiful and a total stranger to wet nappies, childish tantrums and teenage rebellion. He pretends that she has always been remarkably close to her parents, her infancy was one long round of appealing stories and no young man could possibly be worthy of her, let alone heartless enough to disturb this uniquely intimate family circle. He fondly imagines that people believe his nonsense. A stupid paternal pride has blinded him, but he would shudder at any other father who spoke like this, and his guests unanimously shudder at him. His speech is not original, brief, witty or true, but the sorry tradition survives, even flourishes. Hopefully, your culture is not similarly afflicted.

This man, a father for many years and now a father-in-law, returns to normality as abruptly as he departed from it, and a significant friendship develops with the son-in-law he treated with such ignorance in his wedding speech. Fortunately, the eager groom anticipated such drivel, and suffered it with a forgiving pinch of salt. Their relationship progresses naturally towards that of father and son, and proves a vital ingredient in a stable marriage. Friendship, trust, mutual appreciation, practical help and personal counsel flourish readily in the soil of undisguised acceptance where families learn how to accommodate the new family in their midst – the consequence of a marriage, not the conception of a child.

My father-in-law was Jethro. Some knew him as Reuel (Ex 2:18), but on one occasion he sent word to me which unwittingly indicated his own preference: 'I, your father-in-law Jethro, am coming to you with your wife and her two sons' (Ex 18:6). He and I moved quickly from an early hesitancy which tested his natural instincts for hospitality. We soon developed a close relationship in which I valued his wise counsel which managed to be unthreatening as well as penetrating.

When I escaped from Pharaoh's evil clutches, I hurried into the Midian desert where I hoped to keep clear of danger. If you find water in the desert, you stay close to it, and that's what I did. My reading told me that interesting meetings often take place where there's a water supply, and I was prepared to hang around for as long as was necessary while I planned my next move.

The story of Abraham encouraged me. He sent his servant to bring back a wife for Isaac. The canny slave went straight to a spring where he found a stunning young woman for his master's son. 'Rebekah...was very beautiful, a virgin; no man had ever lain with her. She went down to the spring, filled her jar, and came up again' (Gen 24:15–16). The servant asked Rebekah for a drink, and her uncle, Laban, soon hurried back to the spring to offer him our renowned eastern hospitality. '"Come, you who are blessed by the Lord," he said. "Why are you standing out here? I have prepared the house and a place for the camels"' (Gen 24:31). Laban and Rebekah's father, Bethuel, acknowledged the Lord's hand in this meeting, and I was keen to learn from their experience. I too waited at the well, hoping for my own chance encounter.

Before long, an unusual sight came into view, and my heart leapt. Seven young women were approaching the well to draw water for their sheep. I watched them closely, wondering if any of them would trigger my eager chemistry. They didn't seem at all bothered by my presence and went about their business with the skill of experienced workers. But life is hectic where water is concerned. It is a vital source of our life and wealth, and we expect trouble wherever a supply is at stake. The desperate need for water in these arid semi-deserts provokes the selfish violence which lurks in most of us, as I soon discovered when a cowardly group of rival shepherds arrived on the scene. They drove off the women who were powerless to resist their aggression. I knew my own strength from previous

MY FATHER-IN-LAW

fights, and needed no encouragement to play the hero for these attractive ladies by reinstating them at the well.

Unknown to me at the time, these seven sisters returned home with a graphic account of the day's events. Inevitably, their father demanded the full story, not least because he wanted to know why they were home so early. He was a priest, and was only too keen to leave the practical chores to the girls. It's as well I didn't know then that they classed me as an Egyptian, although they had no reason to suspect I was anything else. Breathlessly, competing among themselves to be heard, they gave their dad the details, restricting the report with unusual feminine discipline: 'An Egyptian rescued us from the shepherds. He even drew water for us and watered the flock' (Ex 2:19). Jethro was so protective that he was wary of any stranger who loitered at the well where his daughters were regular visitors. Seven healthy daughters constituted far too valuable a work-force to squander any of them in hasty marriage. At the same time, my actions had aroused his cultural commitment to hospitality, and his questions to his daughters reveal a responsible curiosity: 'Why have you returned so early today?' 'Where is he?' 'Why did you leave him?' (Ex 2:18,20).

Jethro ordered his servants back to the well where they invited me to join them at the family home. It would have been insulting as well as foolish to refuse, and I went gladly. The moment I caught sight of Zipporah, Jethro's eldest daughter, I went weak at the knees. It was love at first sight, and I wondered why I hadn't picked her out at the well. We clicked immediately, and I was thrilled to receive her as my wife. Jethro told me later that he was worried I might prefer one of Zipporah's sisters which would have been very difficult for all of them. In our culture, we expect the oldest daughter to be the first one married, and her father wanted to spare her any humiliation. He needn't have troubled; from the start I had eyes for no one but Zipporah. She knew she had bowled me over, but she decided to play hard to get. She led me quite a dance and gave me a good run for my money, but I was happy to chase her.

A clever girl was my Zipporah. I used to call her 'Zip', because she held the family together in my frequent absences. Jethro didn't like me shortening her name, and he often remonstrated with me: 'Moses, her name is Zipporah.' Once we were married, I ignored his protest, and Jethro smiled grimly, as thwarted in-laws usually do. Zipporah called me 'Mo', which I enjoyed as a pet name. Some of my fellow leaders objected to this on the grounds that she was mocking my public dignity, but that made her do it all the more, a mischievously headstrong woman deflating her husband's pompous colleagues.

I often wonder if Zipporah had any inkling of the pressure my future as Israel's leader would impose on her, but she never failed to be a wonderful and unassuming support to me. Early in our marriage, she did the thing Hebrew husbands most desire of their wives, she gave me a son. I know as well as you do that it takes two to produce children, but we live in a precarious society where a woman's fate hangs in the balance of 'a son or else', and Father accepts no responsibility for the outcome.

We called our first boy 'Gershom', in my paternal recognition that I had been an alien in their land of Midian (Ex 2:22; 18:3). Our second boy, born some years later, was named 'Eliezer'. His name means 'My father's God was my helper' (Ex 18:4). In the first son's name, I pointed to my future mission which would demonstrate how much my life lay with my own people. In the second name, I confessed that this mission had been achieved through the power of God who had saved me from the hand of Pharaoh, and I linked that to the revelation given to me in the burning bush where God appeared as the God of my fathers. Jethro approved of his grandsons' names much more than he did of their parents' pet names for each other.

My father-in-law immersed his life in the priesthood. He loved his work, caring deeply for the people he served and the God he worshipped. His religious experience helped him to appreciate the heavy demands of my calling, and he frequently gave me excellent advice. He kept a close eye on the family shepherding business, but left its day-to-day running to his daughters. He had other pastoral commitments.

As soon as I married Zipporah, Jethro took me into the family firm. I had no father of my own, my Egyptian foster mother was now married and I would be an embarrassment to her, so it was natural for me to become a son to Jethro and he a father to me. He gave me his daughter and he gave me work, both of which were shrewd moves on his part because I could take the sheep further from home than girls dare venture, and he was wise enough to grasp the advantages of another man around the house (Ex 3:1). The deal suited both of us, and we weren't too proud to admit it.

When God broke into my life, he called me to lead Israel out of Egypt. This shattered Jethro's dreams for the future, but he lived so close to God that it did not become a problem for him. One day, I asked to speak privately with him: 'Let me go back to my own people in Egypt to see if any of them are still alive' (Ex 4:18). I wasn't ready yet to reveal more of my historic mission, even to Jethro. In my experience, the best way to keep a confidence is not to restrict it to your close friends, it is to keep it to yourself. I still had some explaining to do, but I marvel at how Jethro waited until I was ready to tell him the full story. He let me arrive at the right moment without rushing me because he knew me and he knew God. He was a man of few words, but they all counted: 'Go, and I wish you well' (Ex 4:18).

Jethro and I never lost contact, and I tried hard to

keep him well informed of our progress. He gleaned news wherever he could, relishing the rumours which flashed around the desert with bewildering speed, while I took pains to see that he heard as much as possible from me. Sometimes Zipporah and the boys accompanied me: 'So Moses took his wife and sons, put them on a donkey and started back to Egypt' (Ex 4:20). Sometimes they stayed with Jethro: 'After Moses had sent away his wife, Zipporah, his father-in-law Jethro received her and her two sons' (Ex 18:2).

We did not spend much time together, but Jethro entered fully into the joy of our worship when God saved us from Egypt. 'Jethro, the priest of Midian and father-in-law of Moses, heard of everything God had done for Moses and for his people Israel, and how the Lord had brought Israel out of Egypt...Jethro was delighted to hear about all the good things the Lord had done for Israel in rescuing them from the hand of the Egyptians...' (Ex 18:1,9). He made a careful study of the way I handled Israel in our wilderness journey, listening attentively to the moans and groans which dogged my footsteps wherever we went; but he never let me know what he was doing. He realised immediately what I was refusing to face: my work-load was too heavy for one man.

One day, I received a message from Jethro that he was on his way with Zipporah and the boys to visit me: 'I, your father-in-law Jethro, am coming to you with your wife and two sons' (Ex 18:6). Do you know the feeling when a simple message leaves you guessing? 'I'd like a few minutes with you.' This is a leadership tactic I often use, playing with people who spend the intervening time anxious to find out if it's good or bad news. For once, the tables were turned on me, and Jethro left me wondering. I'm sure he knew exactly what he was doing, because that's the kind of man he was. There had to be something important on his mind since there was no other way he would risk the long

MY FATHER-IN-LAW

journey to see me. He was not a man to travel far from home if he could avoid it, and I assumed Zipporah had nagged him to help her with the boys. Jethro later admitted that the whole idea was his.

A good clean-up was necessary if Zipporah was coming with her dad, and I tidied the tent very carefully in preparation for the family's welcome arrival. Cultures vary greatly, and you must not react when I tell you that we view such a meeting as man's business. None of your western remarks about male chauvinism, please. Zipporah and I had been apart for a long time, and it was no effort for me to be keen to see her, but it was also natural for Jethro and me to meet first in a public display of affection which later generations may find strange, believing that a man's best welcome should be for his wife. I'm not disputing that, but respect for Jethro as my elder was a prime consideration, and Zipporah was the first to concede it. Jethro and I greeted each other warmly, while attendants ushered away my wife and sons until the important business was complete. Then family recreation took its place. I welcomed Zipporah rather differently from the way I met her father, and she never doubted that she had a healthy husband. Meanwhile, I had thoroughly updated Jethro with our news, and he was thrilled to hear all I had to say of God's blessing. There is something special about a father-in-law's approval (Ex 18:7–9).

Jethro led me in a prayer which was enthusiastic as well as grateful, an act of worship in itself: 'Praise be to the Lord, who rescued you from the hand of the Egyptians and of Pharaoh, and who rescued the people from the hand of the Egyptians' (Ex 18:10). All this time I was asking myself, 'What does Jethro really want?' The wily old bird was biding his time, perfectly aware of my uncertainty about his intentions. The next day he asked me if he could watch me at work, as if he hadn't already done that, and I readily agreed to his company for the day while I judged a variety of dis-

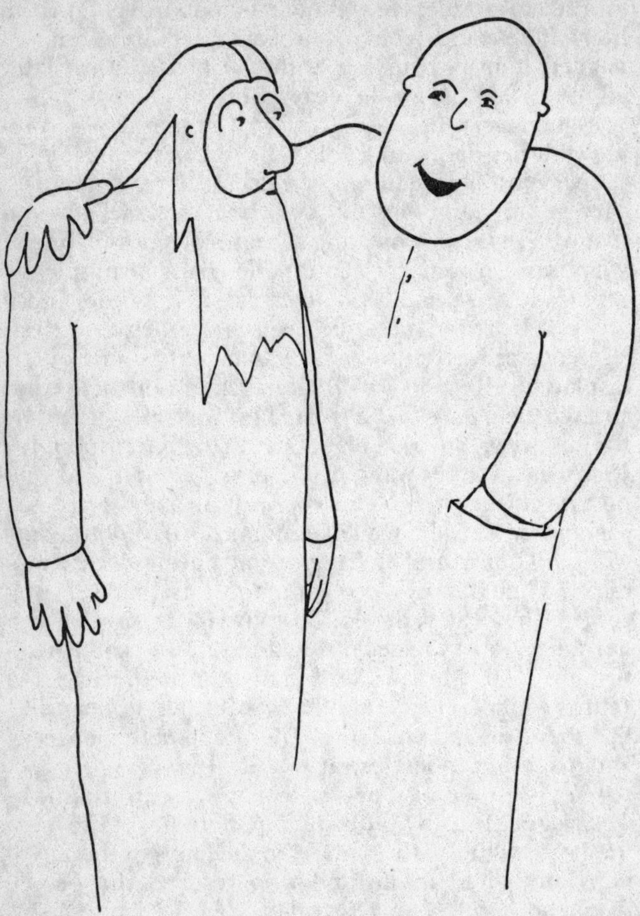

putes for those who needed outside help to solve their differences (Ex 18:13–14). Little did I know that all Jethro wanted was the chance to confirm his suspicions and confront me with irrefutable evidence.

When he felt the time was right, my father-in-law challenged me, always with my interests at heart. He questioned me, while I fidgeted in an obvious desire to justify myself. Jethro cut through it with characteristic penetration: 'Why do you sit alone as judge? What you are doing is not good. You and these people who come to you will only wear yourselves out' (Ex 18:14,17).

Jethro put his finger on the trouble – my need for power and influence, which was resulting in relentless fatigue. No one else could have spoken to me with such refreshing frankness. His idea was infuriatingly simple, as objective counsel usually is, and I was annoyed that I hadn't thought of it first: 'Select capable men from all the people...and appoint them as officials...have them serve as judges for the people at all times, but have them bring every difficult case to you' (Ex 18:21–22). I would remain as sole leader, but many new leaders would share the heat of the day with me. If I could release my people to the care of trusted men, the change would benefit everyone, me above all. Jethro's conclusion summed it all up: 'You will be able to stand the strain, and all these people will go home satisfied' (Ex 18:23). He had more faith than I did that our people would ever go home satisfied, but it all seemed worth trying.

The more I reflect on Jethro's advice, the more I recognise his decisive influence on my life. The lessons he taught me will remain valid. There will be a constant need to discuss issues of leadership, and my experience offers some vital principles for future reference.

(1) If we call people into any form of responsibility, they urgently need to receive trust and training, and

to be made accountable. 'Select capable men from all the people, men who fear God, trustworthy men who hate dishonest gain...teach them the decrees and laws, and show them the way to live and the duties they are to perform...have them bring every difficult case to you' (Ex 18:21, 20, 22).

(2) Everyone must agree where the buck stops. 'You must be the people's representative before God and bring their disputes to him...Have them bring every difficult case to you' (Ex 18:19, 22).

(3) The leader must take enough time to make responsible choices for his fellow leaders. 'Capable men...men who fear God, trustworthy men...listen now to me and I will give you some advice' (Ex 18:21,19).

(4) A clear job description is extremely helpful before anyone starts work. 'Appoint them as officials over thousands, hundreds, fifties, and tens. Have them serve as judges for the people at all times, but have them bring every difficult case to you; the simple cases they can decide for themselves...Show them the duties they are to perform' (Ex 18:21, 22, 20).

(5) Work-load not status is the vital principle when you structure leadership. 'The work is too heavy for you; you cannot handle it alone. Listen now to me and I will give you some advice, and may God be with you' (Ex 18:18–19).

(6) A leader shows his quality more by the way he listens than the way he talks. That is how he learns to assess character with a well-informed and instinctive judgement. 'Listen now to me and I will give you some advice...Moses listened to his father-in-law and did everything he said' (Ex 18:19, 24). I sifted Jethro's motives and realised there was no self-seeking in the advice he offered me; his sole concern was for me and for Israel. He was not manipulating me but sharing his opinion of my best interests. I trusted him, and my trust was not misplaced.

(7) Choose men to be leaders who can work smoothly with a team. Many will give good individual performances which mask their own need for power. Put them into a team of men who expect regular consultation and you'll find out all you need to know. 'Appoint them as officials over thousands, hundreds, fifties and tens' (Ex 18:21). This calls for careful teamwork, but it also offers useful scope for greater and lesser responsibility together with the prospects of promotion for those who do well.

(8) The best leader separates himself not by aloof superiority but by his willingness to make the final decision, to stick to it against all resistance, and to cope with its inherent loneliness. Although valuable counsel came from Jethro, the ultimate responsibility was always mine, and I never conceded my independence. 'Then Moses sent his father-in-law on his way, and he returned to his own country' (Ex 18:27).

If Jethro had been my father, his advice would have threatened me, I would have felt that he didn't trust me to do a good job. If he had been my colleague, his advice would have been a rival bid for supremacy. If the counsel had come from Zipporah, it would have presented itself as unwarranted domestic interference, provoking others to resent the power behind the throne. Only a father-in-law close enough to be honest and distant enough to be unthreatening could have challenged me as Jethro did.

Who knows how closely we might have co-operated or how easily we might have hit trouble if we had spent much more time together? In the mercy of God we found a special relationship which arose as unexpectedly as it continued.

I have introduced this subject of 'father-in-law'. It will lie dormant while people presume they are too busy for the luxury of introspective investigations until a fuller assessment, rooted in the examples of history, provides the material for a fascinating study and even an original doctorate.

I am not ashamed to honour my father-in-law, Jethro the priest of Midian; a man who overcame his initial prejudice; a man with seven shepherdess daughters; a man who loaned, but never fully handed over the best of them to be my wife.

6
The Challenge of Partnership

If you have spent most of your time as top dog, you are not likely to relish the challenge of working in partnership. That's how I see it, after a thorough study of several highly competent leaders. In case you think I'm a pot calling the kettle black, let me assure you that I subject myself to the same scrutiny as I apply to others in authority, and I wriggle as much as they do. The test of partnership sifts your motives, penetrating where no test has gone before, with the result that plenty of leaders crumble in a team who seem to do well on their own.

Perhaps you have worked for many years with no apparent need to consult others, to discuss policy, to submit your timetable or to let them loose up front when you're sure you perform better than they do. You may have faced criticism, but no-one has held power over you. Then other people become equal partners expecting you to welcome their company in the corridors of power. No wonder many men cannot rise to this challenge – which is also a great opportunity to demonstrate the integrity of their own leadership.

I could have been sole leader of Israel for the rest of my life, but I provoked God's summons to proceed in partnership when I resisted his call. He gave me two men as colleagues, one to be my partner and the other my successor. I coped with the former, Aaron, once I accepted the fact that our task needed more than one man; and I coped with the latter, Joshua, as long as I recognised that I was no more than a dispensable servant of God; otherwise I struggled with both of them.

Aaron

Aaron was my older brother by three years (Ex 7:7). He didn't complain about his lesser role as my assistant, at least not in my hearing, but it must have irked him at times, and there were a couple of occasions when he did stumble. I still honour him for the remarkable grace he showed by his willingness to act on a stage where I had the major part. I, who should have been saying, 'I am Aaron's brother,' heard him confess with pride, 'I am Moses' brother.' You won't come across many older brothers who talk like that. God chose his words carefully when he drew Aaron into my call, 'It will be as if he were your mouth and as if you were God to him' (Ex 4:16). Have you ever met a man who is able to play God to his elder brother? No, and neither have I, but it was an attractive possibility. Aaron and I shared the leadership of Israel which God laid upon us and we stuck at it until his recent death, which I mourn greatly, not least because my own departure can't be far away.

Our friendship as brothers equipped Aaron and me to survive most of the ups and downs of a long working partnership. During this time God gave us two sombre warnings. We didn't like what we heard and fought a long battle with depression once the message sunk in: 'For forty years – one year for each of the forty days you explored the land – you will suffer for your sins and know what it is like to have me against you' (Ex 14:34). 'Because you did not trust me enough to honour me as holy in the sight of the Israelites, you will not bring this community into the land I give them' (Num 20:12). In other words: we would wander in the wilderness for forty years, and we would die before Israel went into Canaan.

How would you feel if you had set your heart on the promised land only to be told that you would wander round a desert for forty years, never to enter into Canaan? To us this was bad news. In addition there was the inevitable consequence that Israel needed a successor to me to ensure she did not disintegrate into suicidal anarchy.

It feels as if Aaron only died yesterday. The nation watched us climb Mount Hor, 'and Aaron died there on top of the mountain...The entire house of Israel mourned for him thirty days' (Num 20:28–29). I have collected my thoughts about partnership over many years, but it is only the recent death of my brother which frees me to commit them to paper, so let's do it now while I still have time. I shall separate my partnership with Aaron into three sections, describing each of them in turn. Three headings is a tried and tested method, and I humbly follow the wisdom of the experts.

We came together

We behave naïvely, even stupidly, when we experience a new and exciting relationship. I'm not referring only to courting couples – everyone knows how daft they can be; I'm thinking of many forms of friendship which begin with tremendous enthusiasm. Aaron and I were no exceptions when we became partners as well as brothers. It took me some time to recover from the shock of my call, but I jumped at the opportunity to have a close relative for a colleague. The Lord won my agreement to serve him before he went off to deal with my brother, leaving me to handle my resignation as Jethro's shepherd.

Prompted by the Lord, Aaron and I met in the

desert. We were rarely demonstrative to each other but this time emotion gripped us and we kissed, an unremarkable happening in the East but a bit strange for you (Ex 4:27).

We wasted no time in announcing ourselves to the Israelites, and hurried to start work. I told Aaron all that God had told me and we gathered the national elders to whom Aaron reported everything I had told him (Ex 4:28–30). That was a pattern we often repeated as leaders: I heard from the Lord, Aaron heard from me, and Israel heard from Aaron, which seemed to please the Lord. He stayed with us all the time we obeyed him and rejected compromise. Aaron 'also performed the signs before the people, and they believed' (Ex 4:30).

I did speak in public but it was not my main gift, while Aaron was born with a silver tongue, which is why God put us together. Aaron and I were committed to a unique mission with a distinct prophetic nature. We spoke in God's name as we led Israel along a tough road, but we always gave clear assurance of a great destiny in Canaan. A prophetic role entails public speaking, and that is why Aaron was vital to me, as God had promised: 'You shall speak to him and put words in his mouth; I will help both of you speak and will teach you what to do' (Ex 4:14). I had to be careful; Aaron never bit my head off, but he bristled a few times when I went too far prompting him with noisy whispers: 'Say this'; 'Don't forget to remind them'; 'Have you remembered to let them know?' Although I overcame much of my diffidence, I remained awkward in front of a crowd, leaning heavily on Aaron for the encouragement which meant more to me than he ever knew. I was always clear about what I wanted him to say. We were far more formidable together than we could have been apart – a valuable discovery which lone-rangers need to make for themselves.

Our early days were great for both of us. It's not easy

for two men to share a work which keeps them in the public eye but also demands time alone with God. They are bound to struggle with personal ambition and we certainly grappled with our private temptations. At first we were both so elated that we lived on a high for several months. We were ridiculed by cynics for our honeymoon period, but we didn't object to that. We were impatient to find time for consultation and prayer, discussing at length the most trivial decisions. We spotted the wedges that threatened to divide us, warning off trouble-makers before they could do their damage. We were neither young nor immature; we were brothers pledged to each other and to God, believing in our work and accepting our complementary roles. I was not lacking in natural gifts, but I saw that Aaron's supplemented mine, and I dare to believe he felt the same about me.

We worked together

Part of the reason why Aaron and I made a good team was that we knew God had called us. We offered fierce opposition to Pharaoh, making it clear to him that he had a fight on his hands when he took us on. We wanted to leave Egypt as quickly as possible and were not too bothered about offending him by refusing his unwanted hospitality: 'This is what the Lord, the God of Israel, says, "Let my people go, so that they may hold a festival to me in the desert"' (Ex 5:1). When Pharaoh threw out our request, Aaron's willingness to share the abuse Israel heaped on us expressed a commitment to me which I never took for granted. The crushing increase in our workload as slaves was a terrible blow, but Aaron did not flinch from the fury which came our way: 'May the Lord look upon you and judge you. You have made us a stench to Pharaoh and his servants and have put a sword in their hand to kill us' (Ex 5:21). I'll say more about this when I discuss Israel's incessant grumbling, but I do want to pay tribute to Aaron's unwavering loyalty in those early and formative days.

Any complaints I had to make went straight to the Lord: 'Why have you brought trouble upon this people? Is this why you have sent me? Ever since I went to Pharaoh to speak in your name, he has brought trouble upon this people, and you have not rescued your people at all' (Ex 5:22–23). When we're down, most of us thrust our frustrations at a God who won't dance to our tune. In retrospect, I should have shared these outbursts with Aaron more than I did. I suspect he resented his exclusion, and I paid for it years later.

Many colleagues were involved when God called me to meet him on the mountain, each of them grasping his own role when the Lord included all of us in his address: 'Come up to the Lord, you and Aaron, Nadab and Abihu, and seventy of the elders of Israel. You are to worship at a distance, but Moses alone is to approach the Lord; the others must not come near. And the people may not come up with him' (Ex 24:1–2). These instructions went down well and the people responded eagerly: 'Everything the Lord has said we will do' (Ex 24:3). I went up to receive the tablets of stone and the Lord allowed Joshua to climb higher than the others to further his extensive training as my successor. We needed an experienced man to stay behind with the rest of the people, preferably someone with the necessary authority to settle the constant disputes which marred our progress. Aaron had studied me long enough to know the ropes, and I didn't hesitate to leave him in charge while he enjoyed the temporary responsibility offered by my absence. I set out with Joshua, issuing clear orders to the elders: 'Wait here for us until we come back to you. Aaron and Hur are with you, and anyone involved in a dispute can go to them' (Ex 24:13–14).

My brother and I found mutual strength in co-operation and were at our best when we were busy. If I was alone, I often brooded, wondering if Aaron really was as loyal to me as I had assumed. He must have faced similar problems himself, not least when other people stirred trouble by moaning behind my back in a blatant attempt to drive a wedge between us. We were determined that our mission would succeed, and exploited our family relationship to great advantage. Like most brothers, we had our moments, but anyone who tried to divide us soon found to his cost that our blood was much thicker than water.

The high point of our partnership came when the Amalekites attacked us at Rephidim (Ex 17:8–16). I asked our military commander, Joshua, to take selected men to defend Israel, promising him that I would stand high enough to be visible so that the staff of God in my hands would inspire our troops (Ex 17:9). If I held my hands up, we did well; but if my arms ached too much, we suffered immediate setbacks. I would prefer not to admit this, but I was an aging leader who had bitten off more than he could chew. You try holding your arms in the air for more than a few seconds and see how you feel. I tired quickly, and my partners gave me a stone to sit on so that the army could see me. Aaron and Hur held up my hands, but they must have been itching to take over or at least to do the arm raising in relays. They said nothing when I tired, but stuck closely to God's instructions. I think I drove them mad, but they set aside their legitimate frustration with a stubborn old man because it was a life-and-death situation for us all. They held my arms steady all day until Joshua led our soldiers to victory.

I could have called for a vote to decide whose arms should take the strain; we could have arm-wrestled to find the strongest man; we might have struggled for supremacy, and they might have refused to support me in my silly refusal to delegate responsibility, but they didn't. We all wanted to win the battle more than we wanted personal prestige, and our victory came quickly. Rephidim taught us important lessons about my stubborn stupidity and their loyalty.

We stayed together (just)

The years of our partnership often tested Aaron's loyalty, which is no more than you would expect in view of his lesser role in Israel. We came together, we worked together, but could we stay together? Looking back, I think we played our cards well by resisting the temptation to make extravagant claims at the beginning. We got on with the job. We did not insist that our commitment to each other was stronger than any others, and we were careful not to criticise less intimate forms of co-operation than our own. People who do that are heading for the fall which follows pride, and I have seen some noisy casualties.

We knew that the daily grind of a relentless journey would put the finger on our human weaknesses which inevitably surfaced as insecurity and ambition. Aaron and I were gifted brothers who had inherited similar traits of strong character. These made us a handful for each other, let alone for anyone else who crossed our paths, and we were both susceptible to flattery. The sifting of our partnership found the chink in Aaron's armour, but it also challenged my willingness to be merciful to him. Two incidents illustrate the testing of our relationship.

(i) Family gossip (Numbers 12:1–15). My sister, Miriam, hurt me deeply when she began to gossip with Aaron, at first behind my back and then more openly. You will know from your own family that brothers and sisters are lethal if they put the knife in, and mine were no exceptions. Clearly, Aaron was becoming increasingly fed up with me, and Miriam felt strongly for him in her natural jealousy for a brother she believed was suffering frequent humiliation. They started on my wife: 'Miriam and Aaron began to talk against Moses because of his Cushite wife,' and they moved on to me,

"'Has the Lord spoken only through Moses?" they asked. "Hasn't he also spoken through us?"' (Num 12:1–2). Then the penny dropped: Aaron was jealous of me and Miriam was annoyed that her older brother was playing second fiddle to the younger. She saw me as an upstart, while I was living as if everyone accepted me as God's chosen leader. Ah, the ministry of sisters to keep their brothers humble. Aaron had always been unwavering in his loyalty to me, but I couldn't push my luck too far. He was in league with our sister, although I doubt if he really wanted to swop places with me when the complaints of Israel came pouring in. Jealously protective of her brother's position, Miriam egged him on, behaving more like an ambitious wife than a mutual sister as she drove a thick wedge between Aaron and me.

The Lord watched Aaron, knowing how badly I was hurt. Then he ordered the three of us to meet and resolve our difficulties: 'Come out to the Tent of Meeting, all three of you' (Num 12:4). He condemned Aaron and Miriam for their spiteful attack on me, afflicting Miriam with acute leprosy which he healed only when Aaron begged me to pray for her. The Lord vindicated me, but I marvelled at his wisdom in calling the three of us together without a hint of his intentions. He taught us that we were all his servants and any distinction between us was rooted in justice not favouritism. Somehow, I get the impression that grumblers rub him up the wrong way.

(ii) National idolatry (Exodus 32:1–35). Our second difficulty was harder to resolve than the first. Perhaps I had allowed myself to become detached from the people, and there's no doubt I failed to realise how prone they were to rebellion. Aaron's easy acceptance of their plot was a bitter pill to swallow when I would have bet my boots that he would never betray our partnership. I struggled with resentment against him. Israel's mischievous approach flattered my brother, adding to his frustration in playing second

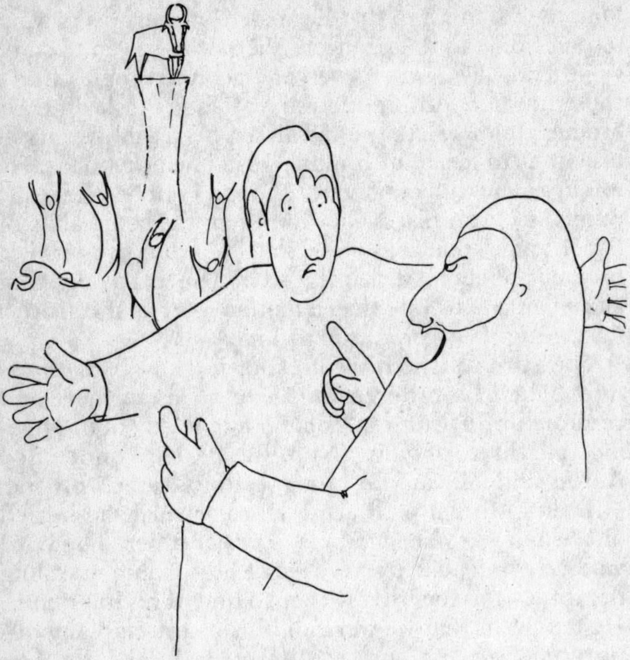

fiddle to me. But this incident also exposed his serious limitations and clarified the Lord's unerring wisdom in holding him back from greater responsibility. The same episode inflicted permanent damage on our relationship.

It's odd how irritated people can get when others are enjoying a long time of worship of which they are not part. I had stayed so long on the mountain with God that those waiting below lost patience with me, seducing Aaron with their idolatrous suggestion, 'Come, make us gods who will go before us. As for this fellow Moses who brought us up out of Egypt, we don't know what has happened to him' (Ex 32:1). My brother quickly agreed to their request, melting the gold from their jewellery to create a calf-idol which they intended to worship. Understandably, the Lord was furious, and I caught the draught of his anger: 'I have seen these people...and they are a stiff-necked people. Now leave me alone so that my anger may burn against them and that I may destroy them. Then I will make you into a great nation' (Ex 32:9–10).

I pleaded with God to spare Israel: 'Turn from your fierce anger; relent and do not bring disaster on your people' (Ex 32:12). He responded by turning Israel over to me, and I acted impulsively, giving vent to the rage which was bursting inside me. It may not have been the most sensible thing to do at my age, but I tore down the mountain as fast as I could, trusting the Lord to protect my heart and my ankles. As soon as I reached the camp, I made straight for the calf-idol and smashed it into the fire, breaking the stone tablets I had brought down from the top (Ex 32:15–16, 19–20). Then I let fly at Aaron. 'What did these people do to you, that you led them into such great sin?' (Ex 32:21). It was a brief question, and I dared my brother to delay his answer. He wriggled in his anxiety to hide his guilt. 'Do not be angry, my lord...you know how prone these people are to evil' (Ex 32:22). (Fancy calling your younger brother 'my lord'! He must have been scared.)

People who won't carry their own cans make me mad. Unlike Aaron, I never felt I could dissociate myself from Israel; perhaps that is the great difference between us. His excuse separated him from the nation; my prayer bound me to it, and I poured out my heart to the Lord: 'But now, please forgive them their sin, but if not, then blot me out of the book you have written' (Ex 32:32). I found that the only way to love Aaron again and find a fresh partnership with him was to pray for him. We were too old to die as enemies. 'And the Lord was angry enough with Aaron to destroy him, but at that time I prayed for Aaron too' (Deut 9:20). Our mutual old age, our dreams of Canaan and many years of effective partnership were enough to pull us together, which shows how important it is to work openly. Aaron and I fell apart because I was away too long and he allowed cunning intrigue to blind him to obvious mischief. We were far more effective working together than apart, despite petty niggles and serious blunders, and our shared mission had to be bigger than we were. Neither of us could avoid these truths, and the fact that we had no desire to do so freed us to find each other again. We learned a lot about ourselves through taking the risk of sharing, even delegating, the responsibility we would have preferred to hug to ourselves.

Joshua

It's hard to contemplate the end of your life's work and the inevitable requirement of handing over to a younger man. In theory it doesn't trouble me. I have often counselled old men who were hanging on too long. But in practice it's not so easy.

God told me that he had chosen Joshua to succeed me: 'But commission Joshua, and encourage and strengthen him, for he will lead this people across and will cause them to inherit the land that you will see' (Deut 3:28). More than anything else, I wanted to enter the promised land, but it was not to be, and I took a long time to accept this dreadful disappointment. Joshua's original name was 'Hoshea', but I thought 'Joshua' was more suitable for a young man who was destined to lead Israel into the security of a new land (Num 13:16).

There is not a great deal to say about Joshua's youth. The few incidents worthy of mention indicate a young man of growing stature, fit to guide the nation at the precise moment on which I had long fixed my sights – which was the time God chose to remove me from the scene.

I have described the way Joshua led the army to victory at Rephidim, when Aaron and Hur held up my arms in support. I say 'the army', but in reality they were no more than a bunch of available amateurs who fought the Amalekites with reckless bravery. This achievement established Joshua's reputation among fighting men for whom military prowesss secures unrivalled respect.

When we approached Canaan, God instructed me to send in spies. It seemed a good idea to use one leader from each of our twelve tribes for this dangerous mission, and this fitted well with the Lord's command: 'Send some men to explore the land of Canaan...From each ancestral tribe send one of its leaders' (Num 13:1). Justice must be seen to be done, the danger was better shared among the tribes, and I won immediate approval for my plan. The tribe of Ephraim picked Joshua for this unique exploration, and I gave detailed orders to the whole team: 'Go up through the Negev and on into the hill country. See what the land is like and whether the people who live there are strong or weak, few or many. What kind of land do they live in? Is it good or bad? What kind of towns do they live in? Are they unwalled or fortified? How is the soil? Is it fertile or poor? Are there trees in it or not? Do your best to bring back some of the fruit of the land' (Num 13:17–20).

I thrust my shopping list at them and they had a good laugh at my outburst of questions. I discovered later that they competed among themselves to find who could do the best take-off of Moses. They were planning to wind me up but realised how upset I was that I was not going with them. The prospect of Canaan had kept me going for years, and I was champing at the bit to explore the country, laying myself open to a pack of practical jokers who would do anything to pull my leg. I would not have put it past them to bring back all sorts of worthless rubbish, pretending that it was a sample of the produce we might expect in Canaan. Fortunately, they took me too seriously to take their pranks too far, and returned with a unanimous report about a fertile country: 'It does flow with milk and honey. Here is its fruit' (Num 13:27).

But our spies did not agree about the natives of Canaan. Ten of them took one view: 'We can't attack those people; they are stronger than we are' (Num 13:31). Only Caleb and Joshua brought a positive assessment which rang with faith: 'We should go up and take possession of the land, for we can certainly do it' (Num 13:30). This provoked a further round of tedious complaints which repeated the incredible view of our slavery in Egypt: 'If only we had died in Egypt...Wouldn't it be better for us to go back to Egypt?' (Num 14:2–3). At last they voiced the conclusion I had long anticipated: 'We should choose a leader and go back to Egypt' (Num 14:4). That would have been the last straw if I had depended on Israel for my security in leadership, but my call came from God, and I determined to keep going.

From the moment of Caleb and Joshua's minority report, I accepted Joshua as God's man to succeed me. He and Caleb refused to join those who plotted against me, openly rejecting every invitation to lead a coup. Outraged by the rebellion which sought to implicate them, they tore their clothes, urging a fickle nation, 'Do not rebel against the Lord' (Num 14:9). 'But the whole assembly talked about stoning them' (Num 14:10).

These two men were willing to suffer for their convictions, and I took due note, sleeping peacefully that night after long hours in prayer for a people who deserved condemnation more than forgiveness. I asked God to pardon Israel while I searched for the assurance of a mercy which changes circumstances. The Lord's answer wrote judgement into mercy, and I knew he had not compromised his holiness: 'I have forgiven them, as you asked. Nevertheless, as surely as I live...not one of the men...who disobeyed me and tested me ten times...will ever see the land I promised on oath to their forefathers' (Num 14:20–23). God chose Joshua and Caleb to lead the way into Canaan: 'Not one of you will enter the land I swore with uplifted hands to make your home, except Caleb son of Jephunneh and Joshua son of Nun' (Num 14:30). I longed to escape the words which cut off my generation from Canaan without allowing me to be an exception.

Now Aaron is dead and my days are numbered. I still have a lot to say to Israel, and I have not minced my words of warning and blessing. 'This day I call heaven and earth as witnesses against you that I have set before you life and death, blessing and curses' (Deut 30:19). Those are my farewell words to Israel; I shall not finish all I hope to say. I summoned Joshua in order to hand over my responsibilities to him, addressing him in front of a hushed crowd who realised they were privileged to be part of history in the making. God urged me to hurry if I still wanted to officiate at Joshua's induction, an occasion I had no intention of missing. If Joshua must take over from me, I would at least be there to crown my own successor. We met, appropriately enough, at the Tent of Meeting in accordance with the detailed instructions God had given me: 'Now the day of your death is near. Call Joshua and present yourselves at the Tent of Meeting, where I will commission him' (Deut 31:14).

You must try my new song. I wrote it for Joshua's induction and it sounded marvellous on the day. But it includes a grim prediction of the spiritual treachery I foresee in the time immediately after Israel enters Canaan. 'I will proclaim the name of the Lord. Oh, praise the greatness of our God! He is the Rock, his works are perfect, and all his ways are just. A faithful God who does no wrong, upright and just is he' (Deut 32:3–4). If that was my beginner's luck, why don't you have a try at writing a song? I found it great fun, even with such a serious message wrapped inside. My effort wasn't short, still less was it a worship ditty to provoke the cynical criticism of boring sceptics who moan at anything new. It accompanied the comprehensive blessing I pronounced on the nation which gathered around me. Then I laid hands on Joshua, seeking for him 'the spirit of wisdom' (Deut 34:9). If my experience was any indication, Joshua would need more than his fair share of anointed wisdom. He'd need his fair share of luck as well. (It's all right, I'm teasing you. I don't really believe in luck any more than you do.) We trembled together in the awesome presence of a God who allowed mere men to bestow his blessing. We were his servants, with neither power nor authority to alter his will. I have nothing more to do; my work is over, and all I want is time to complete this story. Bear with me, and I'll keep writing until my time runs out.

I've already made the point that it is not easy to hand over to a younger man. I am not retiring with relief; God is pulling me off the front line and I am yielding to him. I accept Joshua's role and mine; the one beginning and the other finished, but it demands more from me than I want to give. At the same time, the Lord is with me. He has given me a security in my own achievement and I know he expects nothing more from me. That has renewed my ability to look ahead when my own contribution is over, and not to look back wistfully in unhealthy nostalgia. The Lord called me to trust another man, a younger man at that. The best testimony to my life will not be that everything collapses without me, but that it flourishes under my successor.

Only the Spirit of God can bring a person to the place where I am now; it was never my choice of destination. Trust me, follow me, learn from me and the Lord will bring you that peace of mind as you wrestle with partnership or struggle to accept that it's time to hang up your boots. I have blessed Joshua, believing of my life, 'It is finished.' One day, someone infinitely greater will use the same words of his life (Jn 19:30). My achievements will pale into insignificance by comparison with his, but I feel more honoured than troubled about that (see Hebrews 3:3–5).

7
Coping with Complaints

'If you can't stand the heat you should keep out of the kitchen.' That is fair enough as a comment on the realities of leadership, and I have developed my own self-protection over the years, but I still feel it when the heat is on.

Two aspects of my responsibility have put me under particular stress, and I shall deal with one of them in this chapter and the other in the next. (Isn't 'stress' one of your current in-words? If so, I flatter myself as an old man that I still have something to say.) I want to consider the constant grumbling which has spoilt my years of service, a discussion as relevant to your community as to mine.

Tragically, an undercurrent of dissatisfaction, surfacing as rebellion against God and criticism of me, has hindered our progress. The offenders have never seen themselves as rebels because they fondly imagine that they are upholding something they must guard fiercely; but you will know them by their fruits. Can you expect pigs to do anything but grunt? If the issue was merely a matter of exposing my incompetence, I would have solved the problem years ago by resigning from the job, but the truth has never been that simple. This awful disease of complaint dogs the Lord's people by threatening every genuine work of God and calling into question the integrity of our corporate experience of his power.

When God calls his people to submit to human leadership, he does not impose a tyrannical dictatorship without safeguards, he indicates the best way for community life to run smoothly. True acceptance of God-given leadership creates an incredible peace for all concerned, with much less likelihood of disaster than our unruly scaremongers have been willing to admit.

Unfortunately, grumblers are inevitable companions for those who venture into leadership. They rarely trouble to ensure accurate information because that would challenge their activity; they are quite happy to multiply half-truths and innuendos, oblivious to their own loss of integrity. Aided by lurid imagination, they try to grasp at power they could never wield, while the appointed leader usually does his best to remain scrupulously fair and decisive within the painful limits of his own fallibility. He may live close to God, but he travels a lonely valley of misunderstanding beset by temptations to misuse power and neglect his walk with God. I have been forced to handle the rush of criticism which comes at me through grumbling, and have often been in two minds. When do I listen to it? When do I ignore it? When do I confront it? When can I learn from it? When do I speak and when should I be silent? When do I let on that I'm aware of it? When do I keep my aces up my sleeve, and when do I play them? But this is the heat of the kitchen, and I have lived in it for a long time.

What are complaints?

Almost as soon as I accepted God's call to return to Egypt, I ran into criticism, the beginning of a barrage which has rarely, if ever, relented. When Pharaoh rejected our request to leave his country, everyone turned on Aaron and me. 'May the Lord look upon you and judge you. You have made us a stench to Pharaoh' (Ex 5:21). They blamed us, but they were as much a bad smell to us as they claimed to be to Pharaoh. I know that leaders must bear the brunt of attack when things go wrong, but that still says a lot about the moaners themselves. It's about time we confronted this cancerous blight which eats into communities which are otherwise in good health. It is more than the wicked tactic of a spiritual enemy, it is an instinctive reaction which infects the entire life of any group of people. My study of the years of Israel's grumbling has shown how many parts there are to this malignant growth.

Disobedience

There was a serious outbreak of grumbling against Aaron and me when we entered the desert of Sin, between Elim and Sinai (Ex 16:2). As a result of this obvious dissatisfaction with us, in which we were blamed for every hardship of the journey, the Lord wonderfully blessed us with a miraculous supply of food. He sent it each morning, mysteriously, insisting that we must eat it on the same day, apart from the Sabbath. It might have been easier to deliver it in packets, one per family each day with all the instructions printed on the side. Most people I know prefer to read the side of the packet while they are eating, and this could have been a good use of time. A few small toys for the children to go with the packet would have made a special bonus.

I presented God's word to the nation, adding my understanding of an important judgement: 'You are

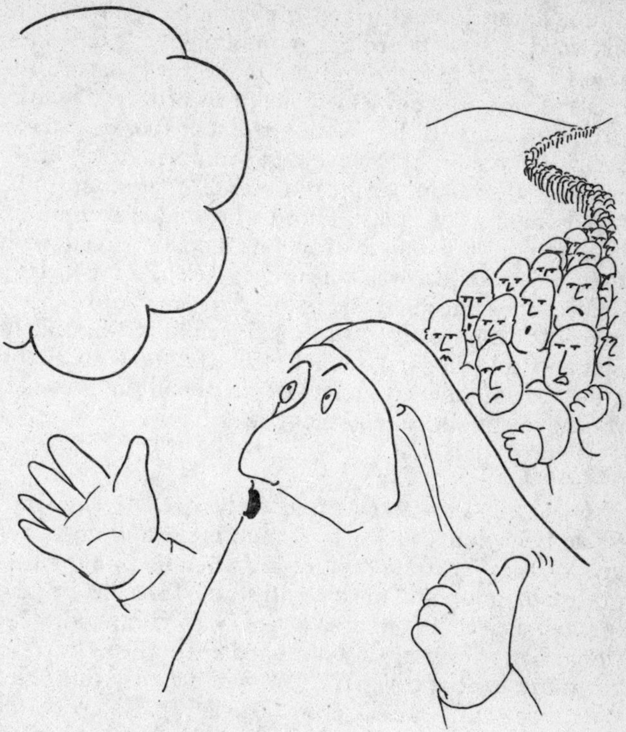

not grumbling against us, but against the Lord' (Ex 16:8). Later, he confirmed my cryptic explanation of his word: 'I have heard the grumbling of the Israelites' (Ex 16:11). Whatever you do, make sure that it's the goals of your journey which dictate its progress, not the problems caused by incessant moans and groans. Learn from our experience that grumbles are an unacceptable distraction from the real task, and you must avoid them at all costs. Those who opposed me paid little attention to my instructions, and God dealt with them in a way that was amusing as well as appropriate. 'However, some of them paid no attention to Moses; they kept part of it until morning, but it was full of maggots and began to smell' (Ex 16:20). How many mints do you have to suck to be rid of bad breath when you have chewed smelly maggots?

Fickleness

History will show how often God's people sink into fickle behaviour. Fickle in commitment and covenant loyalty, they frustrate his blessing when he would much prefer to pour out mercy and love. This has been a further aspect of Israel's tendency to complain. The whole nation promised total obedience to the Lord in gratitude for the covenant: 'We will do everything the Lord has said; we will obey' (Ex 24:7). But you will remember me telling you that when God called me up Mount Sinai I was much longer returning than they were prepared to wait. They were immediately as fickle as they were angry, turning to Aaron and driving a thick wedge between him and me: 'Come make us gods who will go before us. As for this fellow Moses who brought us up out of Egypt, we don't know what has happened to him' (Ex 32:1).

Of course, I blame Aaron, but I also blame those compulsive grumblers who, day after day, crawled out of bed the wrong side. The golden calf they produced for their worship exposed the precarious nature of their loyalty to God as well as to me. If they had any strength of purpose or character, they would have waited for my return, resisted the temptation to complain, refused to be seduced by idolatry, and trusted me to be away only because I had urgent business with God whose sole concern was for their physical and spiritual welfare.

Bitterness

Constant grumbling is symptomatic of a serious spiritual condition which wears a very bitter face. When drought struck us, which is no more than you would expect in the desert, angry murmurs of protest spread like wildfire through the camp which was soon divided against itself but united against me. 'They camped at Rephidim, but there was no water for the people to drink. So they quarrelled with Moses and said, "Give us water to drink"' (Ex 17:1–2). I remonstrated with them but they pressed me harder: 'Why did you bring us up out of Egypt to make us and our children and livestock die of thirst?' (Ex 17:3). They saw me as a scapegoat for their plight, saying with bitter sarcasm: 'Has the Lord spoken only through Moses? Hasn't he also spoken through us?' (Num 12:2). The shoe really pinched here.

Accusation

Accusations fly around as soon as people become dissatisfied. Nothing is more destructive to relationships than these accusing tirades in which fingers point remorselessly at victims they pronounce guilty without trial. Let's remind ourselves of the miracle of spiritual power in which we receive God's forgiveness. We learn there that his mercy cancels all accusations against us and withdraws its judgement, a grace which we must apply to our own relationships. I discovered that living under constant accusation is living in hell; I sank into my deepest depression when people directed mindless anger at me.

A grumbling nation quickly turns on its leaders. We were short of water and very thirsty when we stayed at Kadesh in the desert of Sin, and accusing noises soon made themselves heard against Aaron and me: 'Why did you bring the Lord's community into this desert, that we and our livestock should die here? Why did you bring us up out of Egypt to this terrible place?...and there is no water to drink' (Num 20:4–5). Harsh voices were taking aim, and we were the bullseye for their selfish missiles. As if Egypt was so good, and as if they had any interest in our explanations.

Loss of vision

Once you take your eyes off the goal, you become unwilling to accept the hardships which are inevitable if you are to reach it. We were in the wilderness, but we were travelling to a new life in a promised land. God had assured us of Canaan, and in due course we would come to it. He had saved us by an amazing rescue whose story will live for ever. On our journey we were bound to run into snags, but our shared vision would make even acute setbacks bearable – or it should have done.

Our complaints showed how much we had lost our original vision, turning our complete attention to our sufferings. Our commitment to our vision reveals itself through our attitude to difficulties along the way. The people made their feelings clear to me: 'Was it because there were no graves in Egypt that you brought us to the desert to die? What have you done to us by bringing us out of Egypt?' (Ex 14:11). I must admit, I felt tempted at that moment to find them as many graves in the desert as they wanted. People who talk as they talked the moment they hit problems have lost their vision and may as well give up their whole mission. Our original goal was set by God who had not cancelled his promise: 'I am the Lord, and I will bring you out from under the yoke of the Egyptians. I will free you from being slaves to them, and I will redeem you with an outstretched arm and with mighty acts of judgement. I will take you as my own people, and I will be your God' (Ex 6:6–7). I held to it as the vision of Israel, and I expected hardships on the way. Those who complained had lost their original fire; it was tragic to watch the rot spread through a community which had earlier shown such enthusiasm.

Lies

Complainers have few problems with lies or half-truths. In fact they thrive on them, allowing them to masquerade as established facts: 'Didn't we say to you in Egypt, "Leave us alone; let us serve the Egyptians"? It would have been better for us to serve the Egyptians than to die in the desert' (Ex 14:12). But we weren't about to die in the desert; our conditions in Egypt were anything but 'better', and no, they did not plead to be left alone to serve the Egyptians; that is a lie, a sorry figment of distorted imagination. Sadly, these are the insinuations in which grumblers delight, while leaders wilt under the pressure and try to stem the tide with a reasonable protest, 'But that's not true.'

We had so recently come out of Egypt into the desert of Sin that it astounded me to hear the people moaning: 'If only we had died by the Lord's hand in Egypt. There we sat round pots of meat and ate all the food we wanted, but you have brought us out into this desert to starve this entire assembly to death' (Ex 16:3). Please introduce me to the Israelite family which ever stayed in an Egyptian five-star hotel, because they never invited me to join them for a meal. We may be an opportunist nation, but in Egypt we suffered in an indescribably primitive slave-hole. We certainly did not eat rich food there, and now that we were out of it, we were not about to starve in the desert. But complaints thrive on lies, and the moans of Israel confronted me with a ridiculous view of Egyptian captivity.

Impatience

A good leader soon learns the patience that springs from strong faith. He knows how to hold his nerve when all around him are losing theirs. The ready grumblers waste no time in launching a negative campaign, treating the first problem as a welcome opportunity to sap the national morale with destructive criticisms.

We had crossed the Red Sea, we had gloried in our new hymn of freedom, but now we couldn't find water in the desert, as if that was a tale of the unexpected. A vicious storm of complaint quickly launched itself at me. At the heart of this outburst was a depressing impatience which refused to draw on God's original promise to us. I have always believed that the hurdles ahead of us are there for clearing not stumbling, but maybe no one ever told the grumblers of Israel.

Ingratitude

The blessings of God are not tit-bits of favour wrung from a limited supply of goodwill. They are wonderful expressions of his love given to stimulate our lasting commitment to him. The more we complained, the more we exposed the poverty of our gratitude which was as much a slap in the face to God as it was to me. The people were at it again, moaning so soon after our dramatic rescue from Pharaoh: 'If only we had died by the Lord's hand in Egypt' (Ex 16:3). The Lord must have been sorely tempted to grant their wish. When you are a spiritual leader, you identify as much as you can with the God you serve, and you feel strongly about the criticisms which come your way. You may have given yourself unsparingly, and at times people have been touchingly grateful to you, but you are also rueful about the ease with which that appreciation can evaporate.

Disobedience, fickleness, bitterness, accusation, loss of vision, lies, impatience and ingratitude – all of them are features of the constant grumbling which harassed me on our shameful journey to the brink of Canaan. Those who do complain try to justify their inexcusable behaviour, posing as sweetly reasonable people but infecting a community with a fatal spiritual disease. They blind everyone to the work of God and break the spirit of their unfortunate victims.

How do complaints affect the moaners?

They belittle themselves

Israel began with high hopes, and we can still reach our goal, but we have sunk to a lower one. God chose us to serve him; he heard our Exodus hymn and delighted in it, but the same mouths which gladly praised him have polluted themselves with bitterness. Whenever we grumbled: on the way out of Egypt; in the desert of Shur; in the desert of Sin; by the camp of Rephidim, later called Massah or Meribah; when I was on Mount Sinai; while our spies were reporting on the promised land, we could always have done something else – we didn't have to moan (Ex 14:11; 15:24; 16:2; 17:2; 32:1; Num 14:1ff).

We could have shared a call to prayer; a plea for the encouragement and support of our leaders; a reminder of God's initial promise which had not yet proved empty; a statement of what we must expect in a wilderness journey; a recital of the great deeds of salvation to stir our faith; an imagination of the goal ahead of us; a national brainstorm to help us out of our current dilemma. But we preferred to complain, and we belittled ourselves. As you might expect, we had ringleaders with nothing better to do than ruin a vital mission.

They pollute the whole body

You can't stop grumbling from spreading fast, however hard you try. It hurries relentlessly, infecting the entire community with its foul poison. You can isolate pockets of discontent for a time, but we reached the point where the tide of criticism stirred the whole nation to the act of idolatry which deceived my partner Aaron, offended God – and it began with a grumble (Ex 32). If you want to weed out the grumblers before their influence takes root, you must keep on your toes from the beginning; you can't afford to let anything pass without check. Tell them it's not fair, it's not loving, it isn't even true, and you're having no more of it. They will still moan behind your back, but you won't hear it yourself, and your ignorance will be bliss.

They spoil something lovely

Complaints belong to the darkness and not to the light; they flourish in secrecy but not in openness; they hide behind the back, refusing to speak face to face; they presume on a shameful confidence which is rarely kept, and they spread quickly, breeding mistrust, insecurity and fear. God never intended this for us, which is the reason for my insistence on honest reports and faithful witnesses. 'Do not spread false reports. Do not help a wicked man by being a malicious witness. Do not follow the crowd in doing wrong' (Ex 23:1–2). Our journey should have been a brave pilgrimage but it became a shambles. Thousands of people could have challenged others to have faith for the adventure of risky living. But it didn't happen; we spoilt it all by constant moaning. 'Now the people complained about their hardships in the hearing of the Lord' (Num 11:1). 'Moses heard the people of every family wailing, each at the entrance to his tent. The Lord became exceedingly angry, and Moses was troubled' (Num 11:10).

How do complaints affect God?

We know that God takes a dim view of grumblers. I can

mention three aspects of his displeasure which highlight how much our complaints affect him. (Preachers: a three point sermon if you're stuck for Sunday.)

Rebellion

We direct criticism at those we deem responsible for failure, assuming they deserve our negative comments. Israel used me so much as target practice for her complaints that I almost became immune to the experience. Will we never realise that God calls this 'rebellion'?

A community is right to be suspicious of a man who sets himself too high, and Israel took no risks with Aaron and me: 'You have gone too far! Why then do you set yourselves above the Lord's assembly?' (Num 16:3). But wise caution can also mask spiritual rebellion. The longer we serve the Lord, the more we are tempted to use our maturity as an excuse to denigrate his appointed leaders. God takes a serious view of those who do this, especially when they reject people he has called to great responsibility.

I am treading dangerous ground here, which renders me liable to misunderstanding, but someone has to take the risk in order to sound the necessary warning. The alternative is not to elevate someone above question or to assume that he or she is ambitious for such immunity. The alternative is to allow the Lord to tame us so that we know we're a bunch of spiritual rebels whenever we oppose what he wants. We who believe in our own maturity and expect others to afford our experience due respect, are free to react personally against those who are leaders, but we may find ourselves labelled by God as rebels who deserve his judgement.

Anger

We know all about God's reaction to sexual sin, and we pounce on exposed offenders with malicious glee. But the truth of our Exodus story is that God is equally angry with people who moan their way through life, spoiling themselves and distressing others who have the misfortune to live alongside them. They are experts in self-righteousness, but they fail to convince the Lord. In fact they make matters worse for themselves. God spoke very clearly about this: 'You are a stiff-necked people and I might destroy you on the way' (Ex 33:3); 'How long will these people treat me with contempt?' (Num 14:11); 'Now the people complained about their hardships in the hearing of the Lord, and when he heard them his anger was aroused' (Num 11:1). If God is angry, you'd better watch out; he will deal with those who have sinned against him: 'In this desert your bodies will fall, every one of you...who has grumbled against me' (Num 14:29). Of course he is willing to show mercy, but it's hard to find a grumbler who regrets what he does.

Sadness

We have a lot to learn about our capacity to bring joy and sadness to God, despite the obvious risks of subjective thinking. He formed us for companionship, taking natural pleasure in his creation: 'God saw all that he had made, and it was very good' (Gen 1:31). So much lies hidden in that brief comment, but things soon deteriorated and we have plenty of examples in our own day. 'Miriam and Aaron began to talk against Moses because of his Cushite wife...and the Lord heard this' (Num 12:1–2). It's no surprise that the Lord heard the two gossips, because he never misses a thing. Our records tell us what he thought about them. Our attitudes affect God. We Hebrews are not afraid to ascribe reactions to God which others might dismiss as 'emotional' (you could look up 'anthropomorphic' in the dictionary if you're feeling unusually industrious today). Emotional they may be, but they are neither wild nor irrational, for God is consistent. He is not unmoved by our plight and doesn't stay aloof from us. I would not have been surprised if he had taken Miriam and Aaron and banged their heads together (as a hurt younger brother, I wouldn't have expected much to spill out from either of them). But God was sad; we were failing him by missing the richness of life for which he had called our nation into being, and frustrating his love for us.

I spoke strongly to Israel, bringing her the comfort of the Lord: 'I have indeed seen the misery of my people in Egypt. I have heard them crying out...I am concerned about their suffering...I have come down to rescue them...the cry of the Israelites has reached me, and I have seen the way the Egyptians are oppressing them' (Ex 3:7–9). It is difficult to exaggerate the importance of that communication. The Lord opened up enormous new understandings of himself, removing any limits we might set on his involvement in our lives. Now we face the challenge of meeting human need in the light of God's response to us, which will stretch our concern further than we want. Those who are oppresssed or deprived confront our ease, and we can't wriggle out of a practical response simply because we refuse to link dirty hands with pure faith.

There is a sting in the tail of God's knowledge of our misery; he always knows what's going on. As I see it, that means that the plague of moaning and groaning which has ruined our wilderness journey has moved the Lord. He intended something better for us, and we have blown it. When we complain, we think we sound reasonable, but God hates what he hears. A chosen people who want generous privilege without full responsibility provoke a God who is strong enough to refuse them.

How do complaints affect me?

I'd love to be above the petty scheming around me and

wish I had been constant in my contempt for the moaning which has hounded me, but few people, if any, are as tough as that. Grumbling wastes time and energy, and that makes me mad. Why can't gifted people see through it, even as I have longed for them to hang on to their original inspiration? If I was plotting to destroy God's work I wouldn't need a vast army or a detailed plan; I would sow seeds of discontent in the ears of known trouble-makers, stand back, and watch them spring into life. Before long, the work of God would lie in ruins, which is precisely how we have fared as his chosen people. Gossip, grumbling and criticism have done what Pharaoh couldn't do. Only the strongest leaders and the healthiest communities survive these epidemics of complaint, and even they have suffered some alarming wobbles on the way. The difficulty is that grumblers don't own up. Do you know anyone who has openly confessed, 'I am a nasty gossip with a tongue sharper than the keenest knife'?

I have suffered distress

No man rides criticism without distress and I soon let the Lord know how I felt when I hit trouble: 'What am I to do with these people? They are almost ready to stone me' (Ex 17:4). Their accusations wounded me because they came at times when I thought I was giving to the point where I felt spent, and it is particularly hard to take knocks when you're worn out. A number of people have come into leadership with me, and their eyes have been opened when the firing has turned on them. I rarely missed the chance to remind them, 'I know just how you feel,' not least since a few of them had had a go at me in the past and now looked distinctly uncomfortable; but most of them had the decency to blush.

I was driven to God

Humanly speaking, I was often on the run, defensive

and bewildered. 'All the Israelites grumbled against Moses and Aaron' (Num 14:2). Lack of success threatens the position of leaders, whatever their field of responsibility, but I learned bit by bit to come close to God. He stirred in me the memory of my call so that it lived again. I accepted his assurance, relived his rescue and felt once more the wonder of his promise of Canaan. Whenever God dealt with me, he refreshed me with the confidence that our business was not finished, and I kept going.

I felt hounded

Grumblers demand the best from their leaders but sap their energy to produce it. The more they harangued me, the less I was able to deliver the goods. Those of you who think you are good counsellors will do well to study God's method with me. When Pharaoh pursued us after his second thoughts on our freedom, the people turned on me with their customary gentle understanding. How would you help a man who was hounded as they hounded me? If you counsel someone and want him to appreciate you, you offer comfort and sympathy. You talk to him about his self-worth, pray inner healing into him and even mention obedience to God, provided you don't push him too hard. If you're not gentle enough, he'll find someone else who is, and that's the end of your jealously guarded reputation. It's one thing to have a few faults, but quite another to be known as a poor counsellor.

God used a different method with me, and it didn't take long: 'Why are you crying out to me? Tell the Israelites to move on' (Ex 14:15). He had me in and out of the counselling room before I could sit down, let alone make myself comfortable. I don't think he even gave me the chance to close in prayer, it all happened so fast. I went to him rueful, looking for all sorts of comforting ministry, but the Lord picked me up, dusted me down, slapped my backside, and told me to get on with it; everything my counselling manuals have told me not to do. But God's way works, and it saves time.

I found a team of colleagues

Jethro advised me to gather a group of trusted men and to delegate specific authority to them. This enabled constructive criticism to be made within a relationship of mutual commitment. It didn't solve all our problems overnight, but it did establish a forum where a solution became more likely. If we shared responsibility, we would share everything else, including the sting of complaints. We were determined to finish the job, and that helped us stay together even when we had flare ups. I admit, reluctantly, that it was the complaints Jethro heard which persuaded him to counsel me to find help, and I praise God for my father-in-law's insights and his courage to press them on me.

So what will you do with your moans and groans? Why don't you start with an apology to your leader and a specific word of encouragement to send him or her on their way? The compliment might be returned to you, and that would be even better. No, don't tell me pigs might fly; that would make you a cynic as well as a grumbler, which won't help anyone.

There's been plenty of teaching material in this chapter, but my experience is that once you have introduced the subject, the known complainers among you will look at you with injured innocence, wondering what on earth you're driving at. Then they go home to moan about your lesson. Don't say I haven't warned you.

8

Coping with Myself

The grumblers and moaners among us made life difficult for me, but the demands of my work meant that I was not always a piece of cake to handle. The obvious difficulties I faced were rebellious exiles, a stubborn Pharaoh, tribal organisation and rivalry, and an acute shortage of supplies with regular famine and drought – all complications of our long journey. But I also wrestled with the stress of a pressured job which restricted my freedom.

Israel was disgruntled with our meagre desert rations, and I faltered when the scorching sun sent temperatures sky-high. The people harked back to Egypt and, for a moment, I wondered if we had done the right thing in leaving. From that time, I kept my doubts to myself, knowing that my defence had become shaky. I was too emotional in temperament to ignore persistent criticism, and I struggled with a burning desire for revenge.

I won't bore you with a blow-by-blow account of every crisis, but I will confess my battle to maintain public respect in the face of pressures which threatened to destroy me. It will do me good to admit what happened, and it won't do you any harm to recognise yourself in me. Please accept my apologies if you've suffered a recent battering from predictable preachers, but I have isolated three things from my personal struggle. To soften the blow of another three-point sermon, I'll divide the second of them into four headings – a master-stroke of initiative and originality.

Temper

I was born fiery and I stayed that way. During my early years in Egypt I took full advantage of my royal privileges, especially if I wanted to push other boys around. I knew my own strength and dared them to resist me. Child experts, steeped in the famous Egyptian wisdom, watched me from a safe distance, shook their heads and concluded, 'This boy is disturbed;' as if it required extensive research to yield results which were already obvious to the palace nannies on whom I inflicted a torment my Hebrew mother never had to endure. I was not disturbed, but I was coming to terms with two things: unusual physical strength and the traumatic circumstances of my adoption; my real parents desperately wanted to keep me.

As you know, my mother did try to maintain contact with me. She taught me to speak Hebrew to prevent me from changing into an educated Egyptian who was a stranger to his roots. She also fed me detailed information about the plight of the captives. The whole process made me uncertain as well as angry, and I became a big handful to those who were responsible for me, despite the faithful love of my Egyptian mother, the princess daughter of Pharaoh.

In time I brought my emotional turmoil under a measure of control. My education in Egypt was a marvellous advantage, and I hid my Hebrew indignation until I had an opportune moment to unleash it. That long-awaited day dawned with no warning of its impending drama. I wandered out to a place I knew well, combining useful exercise with cautious interest in the slaves who were working there. I took no conscious decision on that fateful day, I just boiled over. There was nothing I hadn't seen many times before, but this time it was too much. I spotted an Egyptian thrashing a Hebrew. Glancing round in all directions, I tried in vain to stifle a rising fury. It sounds straightforward in our records, but the truth was violent and bloody. I 'killed the Egyptian and hid him in the sand' (Ex 2:12).

It's impossible to remember all I felt that night. I was scared, angry and excited, all at the same time. The euphoria of revenge and the fear of detection met in wild panic; I had killed a man. I tried to sleep, but when I closed my eyes I saw fingers pointing and eyes staring in stark accusation, 'Murderer.'

The next day, in a pretence of normality, I went for my usual walk. Two Hebrews were fighting and, on impulse, I intervened. All I wanted was to save them from themselves, but they resented my intrusion. One of them stuck his face into mine and, snarling, put the question I dreaded: 'Are you thinking of killing me as you killed the Egyptian?' (Ex 2:14). I had lost my temper, committed murder, and my secret was out. I fled immediately into the Midian desert and Pharaoh set a price on my head which made the obvious point that my adopted link with Egypt was finished. I was now a Hebrew and not an Egyptian.

That's not a new story to you, but I need to tell it to underline my terrible temper. I've lived with my own violence, and I suspect I'm not the only person who has found it difficult to control himself, but at least I've tried.

A sharp temper is not always a bad thing, although it is a handicap. What kind of man would ignore the sufferings of his people? I'm not trying to justify what I did, but the Egyptians treated Hebrew life as very cheap and they needed a dose of their own medicine. Frankly, I'm proud I was not a coward when I found that Egyptian bullying one of my countrymen, and it made me mad to find two Hebrews destroying each other when they must have known that cruel masters who sneered in contempt whenever slaves had a fight, would dish out severe punishment for it. At the same time, my temper was far too quick. Something had to be done about it.

This temper served me well in the Midian desert when the hooligan shepherds attacked Jethro's daughters at the well where they were drawing water for their father's sheep. The girls were attractive as well as skilful, and I rescued them from aggressive cowards in a display which combined chivalry with temper. I knew I was strong, and made short work of the desert thugs with the welcome benefit that I impressed eligible young ladies in the process. My temper won me beautiful admirers and a lovely wife, Zipporah, the gift of her relieved father, Jethro. Protective instincts, righteous anger and a quick temper made me a formidable opponent on more than one occasion, and I enjoyed my reputation too much.

God's call for me to lead Israel produced no instant changes in my temper. I battled on, trying to master it before it ruined my work. Uncontrolled outbursts were a luxury I could no longer afford. People wanted to trust me, but found me too unpredictable for comfort. God took me in hand, but my lapses caused me frequent remorse and occasional humiliation. At times Zipporah and the boys were apprehensive, until I sorted myself out. One morning I overheard her say to Gershom, 'Now be careful this morning with your father. He's very tired, and when he's tired he's irritable. Mind what you say to him.' Fancy hearing your wife talk like that. I determined to be gentle that morning if it killed me. I waited several days before letting on that I had eavesdropped on their conversation, and we all laughed about it. But it made me realise that one man's temper is expensive for a lot of people. Listen carefully to your family's whispers, as I did. A wife's motherly counsel is sobering stuff for her husband to overhear.

Inevitably, Israel's persistent ingratitude has upset me by inflicting the moans of petty visionless men who don't care whether their scurrilous poison is true or not. It would have been easier to give the moaners a good hiding to instil a healthier respect for their leader. Reluctantly, I recognised this as a short cut I dared not take, but it tempted me many times. It has cost me dearly when I've let my fists do the talking, knowing above all that I have failed the Lord. Only people with my kind of problem can appreciate the misery of failing when you most want to succeed; when your temper damages those you least want to hurt; when you sense what the Lord feels and you long to try again. It is a shattering blow each time it happens, and you wonder if you can ever make up the deficit. You try to hide, in fear rather than shame, but it doesn't work. At times you despair. Will you ever win? Are you the only one who is a helpless victim of his own temperament? Is your childhood producing an angry young man whose foul temper will always limit his achievements? Or, can God change you – soon?

Perhaps the Lord noticed the raw materials of a promising leader in me. He met me where I was, harnessing my potential and taking time with me. He dealt patiently with my temper, using well-tried methods which introduced doubts about my behaviour, made it harder for me to justify myself, convicted me bit by bit that this must not continue, and stimulated compassion and regret for those who had suffered the lash of my tongue and the brutality of my fists. He led me to confess my temper and plead for help; then we were in business.

Do you have similar problems with your temper? No, don't immediately think of someone else. Answer the question for yourself and see if the family agrees with your conclusion. If you face up to the truth, you'll be well on the way to progress, otherwise your temper will hold you back from a bigger contribution to God which will be as great a pity for you as it threatened to be for me. You can win if you really want to, but it will entail lots of prayer, plenty of heartache, and honest encouragement from people who love you.

Pressure

'Pressure' is a new word for me, but it's probably jargon for you, and I want to rush in with a contribution to ensure my early arrival on the bandwagon. Heavy pressures have been a feature of my working life. It's difficult to pin them all down, but you know the symptoms: you can't relax; you talk nothing but work; you go to bed with your mind racing and wake up convinced you haven't slept a wink all night; people plead with you to take a break and you refuse angrily instead of accepting gratefully; your jokes are more laboured than usual and the only people who laugh are those who are afraid of upsetting you if they don't; you insist you're not hungry but you know you're not eating; you're like a cat on hot bricks and a bear with a sore head at the same time. You can refuse to call a halt, but the only sure thing ahead of you is a breakdown.

This business of pressure has a spiritual dimension. I have been God's man, doing God's work for God's people, and the pressures on me were calculated to spoil everything. An unseen enemy sought to frustrate our progress, stirring constant complaints for which I was the favourite target. The question was straight enough: 'What have you done to us by bringing us out of Egypt?' (Ex 14:11). I replied with the full truth: we were in God's hands, we were following his purpose, and he would respond whenever we called on him. 'Stand firm and you will see the deliverance the Lord will bring you today...The Lord will fight for you, you need only to be still' (Ex 14:13). I coped with pressure when I kept my confidence in God. If Pharaoh opposed me, he opposed God, not because I was any great shakes but because God put me where I was and stayed with me. I've proved this principle of godly leadership many times. My experience shows that God is utterly faithful in his pastoral care. He always knows what he'll do, but he doesn't feel bound to tell us the moment we demand full information from him.

I won't impose an overdose of introspective agony on you, but I will mention those pressures which have been hardest to handle. They will affect your leadership as surely as night follows day, although many alleged pressures are euphemisms for 'temptation', but they win us more sympathy when we call them 'pressures'.

The pressure to give up

You know that Aaron and I met trouble when Pharaoh refused to allow us time off for a desert festival. He demanded as many bricks as before, but ordered us to fetch our own straw from now on. He was vicious, and he knew it. Bitter slaves rounded on us, blaming us for their predicament: 'May the Lord look upon you and judge you' (Ex 5:21). That was tantamount to a curse, and I was tempted to give up. This kind of treatment was not part of my original contract and I wondered why everything was going so wrong. Must I tolerate personal abuse for the rest of my life?

But God dealt with me. The more I churned inside, the more he strengthened my resolve to carry on. If you are in the right, you're in the right. If you have heard God speak, you've heard God speak, whatever the reactions to your decisions. I didn't resign, I dug in. 'Look where you've got us now' is an old trick of worthless grumblers. It must cut no ice when you serve the Lord.

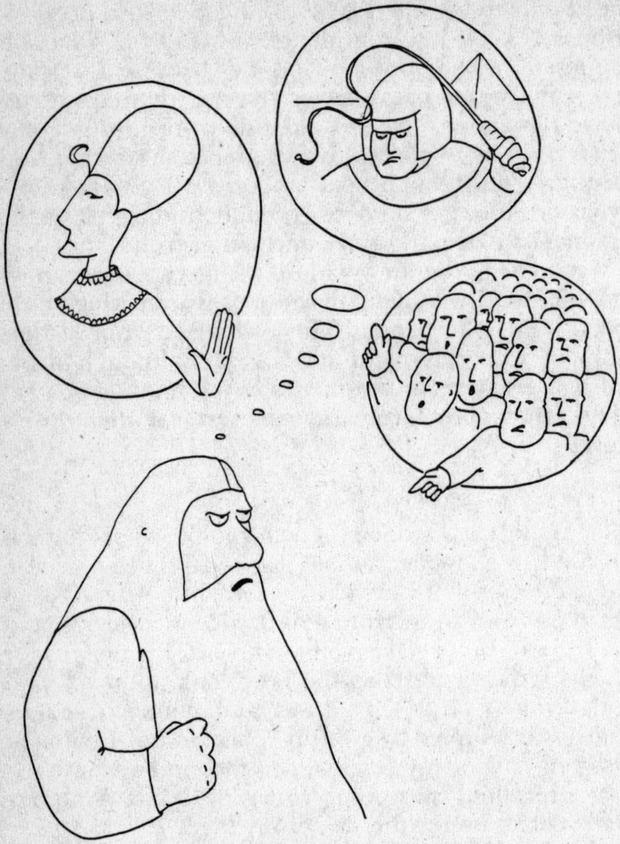

I was not too troubled when the people wanted to replace me. They had picked the wrong man to sack; only the spineless cave in at the first setback, but my backbone's fine. Most of the spies who returned from exploring Canaan gave a pessimistic view, and Israel took it out on me. 'Wouldn't it be better for us to go back to Egypt? We should choose a leader and go back to Egypt' (Num 14:3-4). The Lord took the wind out of my sails when he refused me any sympathy, demanding instead that I sympathise with him. 'How long will these people treat me with contempt?' (Num 14:11). It was a telling reminder that it was his work and not mine which was at stake. I stayed in the job because I was convinced of spiritual realities; my call, Israel's destiny, and the knowledge of a living God whose hand was upon me.

The pressure to turn back

The pressure to turn back met me when we were only six weeks out of Egypt ('the fifteenth day of the second month after they had come out of Egypt' [Ex 16:1]). Six weeks from a dramatic rescue, six weeks into an incredible journey, and we were voicing a death wish at the first obstacle: 'If only we had died by the Lord's hand in Egypt' (Ex 16:3). The possibility of such weakness had never entered my head, not even in my worst nightmare, and I was badly shaken. Only a bunch of weak-kneed wimps could contemplate retreat as quickly as we did. The people had blamed me for Pharaoh's chase, and I realised then how easily they would talk of turning back, but it was not a serious option in my book. Now we had crossed the Red Sea and I had to think fast. They were at it again, hankering after a return to Egypt because we were short of water. Did they really think a new Egyptian army would welcome them home with open arms? 'Come back Israel, all is forgiven!'

Once you have made up your mind to leave a situation, and have declared your faith for the journey, you cannot turn back. God drove this point home when we fled from the pursuing army of Pharaoh: 'Tell the Israelites to move on' (Ex 14:15). The enemy followed us into the sea but never reached dry land, and we dared not contemplate turning back. It was an amazing sight when God struck the Egyptian army. Their chariots swerved in chaos as if we had laced their drinks with a lethal Semitic brew.

How could we suggest turning back so soon after a moving commitment to go ahead? 'And when the Israelites saw the great power the Lord displayed against the Egyptians, the people feared the Lord and put their trust in him and in Moses his servant' (Ex 14:31). God had kept his word, not as a temporary boost but as an act of total integrity. If the people had asked positive questions in our water shortage they would have received answers which ruled out the possibility of turning back.

The pressure to renounce God

Often, when you most want God to speak, he seems silent, distant, and strangely indifferent. He hasn't done things according to my timetable or my ways. Food from heaven; water from the rock; a dry sea-bed; victory by arm-raising and guidance by cloud and fire are all very well, but they hardly enhanced my reputation for competent strategy, and you cannot presume on miracles appearing to order. I sided with God against his people, but I ran the gauntlet of my own doubts which circumstances frequently intensified. I did not cave in because I believed he was still with me, whether I felt it or not. I kept going and discovered further surprises of his love.

The pressure to lower my standards

National leaders in a tight squeeze are bound to come under pressure to secure advantages by lowering their standards. I did, and I'm not the only one by a long chalk. The pressure comes from the temptation to use your position to further your own ends; it's always been a sticky one for those in high office. Fortunately, I've read my Joseph and have stayed on my guard for 'Potiphar's wives'. It's easy to sink into corruption, because you're never short of willing assistants who are facing similar pressure and who covet the benefits which your favour can bring. The pressure of compromise is subtly disguised and never withdraws its seductive invitation.

My wife, Zipporah, spent a lot of time away from me (sorry, I spent a lot of time away from her), which meant that attractive alternatives were at hand to replace her. Many people wanted my attention, and I would have been less than human if their willingness had no appeal for me. The pressure was there to lower my standards and to indulge my masculine appetite, but that would have destroyed the moral basis of our mission. Any form of immorality on my part would have an immediate effect on colleagues who looked to me for an example – and for a hint that they could snaffle a few easy perks on the side.

I represented Israel to God, and I came to the nation in his name. The more aware I was of this priestly life, the closer I walked with the Lord who gave me fresh insights into the implications of his holiness. A holy God is not content to be different from men, he summons them to be like him: 'Be holy, because I, the Lord your God, am holy' (Lev 19:2). Moral compromise beckoned to me all the time, but I owed it to myself, to my family, to Israel and to the God who trusted me to resist the pressure. I speak more in relief than pride that I survived intact, confident that you won't find skeletons in my cupboard. But it was tough for me, and it won't be easier for you. If God puts the reins of leadership in your hands, you'd better stay awake;

there are plenty of people who will be happy to put you to sleep.

Discouragement

I found our hardships, our grumbles and the grinding heat of a remorseless journey very discouraging. I tried to keep this to myself, but too many people were watching me for a hint of a change of mood. Aaron and I were friends as well as brothers (most of the time), and we supported each other. We both suffered from a mixture of despair and frustration, but my certainty of God's call strengthened me to believe we would reach Canaan, eventually. That confidence overcame the depression which hounded me, and God made me strong.

Pharaoh's continuing awkwardness in the negotiations surrounding the plagues was terribly wearing. Time and again I thought we'd clinched our freedom, only to have our hopes dashed by a fresh refusal to let us go. It didn't help me to be surrounded by jostling reporters every time we left Pharaoh, each of them frantic for an exclusive bulletin or a mischievous quote. Pharaoh discouraged me, but I saw we would wear him down in the end. I refused to alter my terms because I knew I was in the right. God's clear commitment to our struggle helped me keep my nerve, and we Hebrews always strike a hard bargain. Those who let discouragement swamp them find it hard to see a world beyond themselves, but I tried to look out, knowing that Pharaoh was growing desperate. He resisted me but he did not change me.

When you are opposed by people who have the power to dismiss you, do not allow them to weaken your resolve to finish the job you started. It was pretty awful when Israel ganged up on Aaron and me after Pharaoh's initial refusal to let us leave Egypt, and I told the Lord just how I felt: 'O Lord, why have you brought trouble upon this people? Is this why you sent me? Ever since I went to Pharaoh to speak in your name, he has brought trouble upon this people, and you have not rescued your people at all' (Ex 5:22–23). If you want a perfect statement of discouragement, there it is. But I carried on, and so must you.

Bitter recriminations accompanied the water shortage at Rephidim, and I deflected the anger to the Lord, but it was I who came low when he challenged me: 'Why do you quarrel with me? Why do you put the Lord to the test?' (Ex 17:2). Is discouragement really a form of unbelief? I suppose it is, but at least God answered me. I cried out to him, 'What am I to do with these people? They are almost ready to stone me.' He replied firmly, 'Walk on ahead of the people...' (Ex 17:4). His counsel of immediate action was a timely breath of fresh air and a good kick in the right place – just what I needed. We obeyed him and found water.

'I am the Lord...and I will bring you to the land I swore with uplifted hand to give to Abraham, to Isaac and to Jacob. I will give it to you as a possession. I am the Lord' (Ex 6:6, 8). I reported this to the Israelites but they refused to listen 'because of their discouragement and cruel bondage' (Ex 6:9). When I rode high on the promise of God, Israel's cynicism threw me to the ground. Don't you find that the cold apathy of those you lead can crush your enthusiasm, especially if it is born out of their discouragement? It's devastating, but we learn to expect these blows among the harsher pressures of leadership.

I knew how down I was when God sent me back to Pharaoh against my will. 'Since I speak with faltering lips, why should Pharaoh listen to me?' (Ex 6:12). That was defeatist talk, and I had to toughen up before God could use me. Positive truth pressed on reluctant ears rarely secures a good hearing. I was suffering from a peculiar deafness, not listening to the words I most wanted to hear, even as slavery, oppression and abuse had reduced Israel to a despair which didn't respond to the truth. Discouragement paralyses your mind; it freezes fresh initiatives; and prevents good ideas from coming to birth. It's like an intruder creeping in when you least expect him and possessing you before you realise what's going on. You struggle to free yourself from the grip of a black mood, succeeding only if you give it your best shot. I won when I refused to submit to discouragement, but I suffered some nasty accidents on the way.

Perhaps I should confess to you that I was occasionally baled out by my anger. I can't pretend it was always righteous anger, although that's not what I claimed at the time, but its effect was positive. Did I sin or not? If I had not reacted with fury when I found the calf-idol in our camp, I would have crashed into complete discouragement. The Lord was also angry: 'I have seen these people, and they are a stiff-necked people. Now leave me alone so that my anger may burn against them and that I might destroy them' (Ex 32:9–10). If I was angry, was my anger less righteous than his? That's what I told my boys whenever I dished out paternal discipline and they teased me about the sin of anger. They refused to accept my point, but by that time we were sharing a good laugh, and the conclusion wasn't important.

God called me to a bigger responsibility than I ever envisaged or felt competent to accept. He tested me in ways I could not foresee, exposing me and putting my faith on the line. That subjected my marriage to a searching examination, which usually happens when God leads men and women into special service. Husbands and wives who have jogged along happily for many years, wonder what has hit them when God pulls them into a new sphere of service which puts their marriage on the line. Instead of blissful partnership, new tensions arise without warning. The problems Zipporah and I met were no different from those other leaders have faced. We laughed privately when they confided in us on the assumption that their troubles were unique, and we made it obvious that we'd experienced almost everything they were talking about. Most of them needed nothing more than that knowledge together with my reassurance of full confidence in them and my prayer for God's protection over a marriage which still had a great deal going for it. Others were in a more serious condition. But who gave them the idea that Zipporah and I were immune from pressure?

I have discussed the pressures of leadership as they have affected me; they may not be the same for you. They have challenged me, and I have only survived because I've drawn heavily on spiritual resources which need constant renewal. If I have served God, the ultimate privilege is mine, but any honour belongs to him. You may think I've made a big mess along the way, and you're right, but that's nothing compared with the chaos I would have left behind if God had not been patient with my pilgrimage of temptation and faith. He'll be the same for you, if you launch out when he calls you.

9
Our Experience of God

The poets, prophets and story-tellers of Israel will take centuries to complete a marvellous collection of writings, the heart of which will be God's saving rescue in the Exodus. We prefer to speak of God in practical ways, leaving intellectual speculation to other nations yet to be born. My offering to you is typically Hebrew – a description of God's character through his activity in our lives which is like digging into a huge mountain where even the first barrow-loads overflow with rich soil.

I've no more seen God than you have, but I've met him so dramatically that it feels like I've seen him; it was everything but a face-to-face encounter. The fact that no one can see God physically has made our people quick to envy the paganism of local religions. These have turned to grotesque or extravagant idols which have seduced them with the illusion that they represent God in a visible form. You and I can dismiss that as nonsense, but how do you convince a fickle nation which demands a tangible expression of its deity? It's a pretty safe bet that we are in for a long struggle over this issue. It will become a life-and-death issue for the prophets, and a sizable contribution to the writings of our faith. Future generations will be in no doubt as to where I stand on the matter: 'Break down their altars, smash their sacred stones, cut down their Asherah poles and burn their idols in the fire. For you are a people holy to the Lord your God' (Deut 7:5–6). As if you can confine God in a lump of wood or metal! But Israel is reluctant to face that.

In these early days of Israel, we are looking to establish convictions of faith and patterns of life which will secure a lasting influence on the nation. Mine is not the last word on the subject, but it does highlight God's impact on the incredible adventure of my life. The more you catch its wonder, the more you will venture out, trusting God even when he leads you where you do not want to go, as he has led us.

God has made us a nation, holding us together when we would otherwise fall apart. My exploration reveals contrasting attitudes towards neighbouring religions, sometimes of narrow aloofness and sometimes of blatant plunder. It concerns me greatly that unabashed paganism so easily infiltrates our Hebrew faith, its degrading practices negating the core of our belief. For that reason, I want to record my understanding of the God who has revealed himself to us, above all through the Exodus from Egypt. My account will consider vital aspects of his revelation and our response.

The holiness of God

'I, the Lord your God, am holy' (Lev 19:2). I believe that holiness is the most important statement we can make about God. It is difficult to explain God's holiness in a way that does not make him remote. We have some things in common with local religions, but the gap between us will widen quickly as the Exodus theme takes control of our faith, not least in the ways we describe God. Only a degenerate Israel will contemplate a return to the religions we left behind us, and that is a battle I gladly bequeath to my distant successors. They will struggle for a fuller knowledge of God's holiness in a time when Israel will be content with the correct performance of ritual requirements.

The root meaning of holiness is 'distance'. When God called us to meet him on Mount Sinai, he warned us to keep our distance. 'Come up to the Lord, you and Aaron, Nadab and Abihu, and seventy of the elders of Israel. You are to worship at a distance, but Moses alone is to approach the Lord; the others must not come near' (Ex 24:1–2). He had already promised to meet me on the same mountain ('I am going to come to you in a dense cloud' Ex 19:9), and he fixed rigid boundaries for the rest of the people. 'Put limits for the people around the mountain and tell them, "Be careful that you do not go up the mountain or touch the foot of it. Whoever touches the mountain shall surely be put to death"' (Ex 19:12). Regulations for the Tabernacle allowed only the Levites to care for it, to touch it or to move it. They were made 'holy' for their task by their separation from the rest of Israel. 'The Levites are to be responsible for the care of the Tabernacle of the Testimony' (Num 1:53). We have specific regulations about what the Levites can wear, and they have to keep themselves scrupulously clean; no mean feat where we live (Lev 16:4).

Such practices may seem strange and even superficial to you, but they mark the vital beginning of an idea of God which will develop into something with wonderful implications for Hebrew worship and morality. However, we must not allow this early understanding of God to fossilise, but must welcome the unfolding of further truths about the Lord.

When God formed Israel as a nation, he wanted us to be holy, which means 'reserved' for him. 'For you are a people holy to the Lord your God. The Lord your God has chosen you out of all the peoples on the face of the earth to be his people, his treasured possession'

(Deut 7:5–6). It is an amazing privilege as well as a daunting responsibility to reserve yourself for God. I've seen traders slap 'reserved' on goods in the market to keep them for shoppers anxious to have enough money for all they want to buy but unwilling to lose a good bargain. It's funny as well as scary to imagine God at work in Israel, fixing reserved signs on us to claim our exclusive allegiance. It is an important marriage between responsibility and privilege.

We are putting into words something uniquely powerful about God's character when we call him 'holy'. I felt it when he called me, which partly explains why I held back. The familiar scenery unnerved me that day; his compelling presence silenced me, and an eloquent hush warned me to do nothing until I was willing to do everything. Speech may be silver, but this silence was golden. The dirt of the day's shepherding was on my shoes which he told me to take off, and my bare feet became a symbol of my nakedness before a holy God, a reminder that I had no secrets from him. I kept my distance while God revealed the meaning of his holiness, yet I felt an irresistible urge to approach him. That is the paradox of God's holiness. Precise regulations I have faithfully communicated to Israel require us to keep our distance, but they also provide for someone to draw near. One day, God will remove this separation, creating a wonderful new way for us to be near him with confidence, and that will confirm not compromise his holiness.

It will take us a long time to master the meaning of holiness, and we must be patient. When a baby begins to feed, it can only manage milk but it moves naturally to an adult diet. This process is applicable to Israel as we try to understand God. Some of our early ideas may disturb you as strange, even alien, but they are important for the initial stages of our journey. They highlight the greatness of God and the awesome wonder of knowing him. They provide points of contact as well as of departure when we compare our Hebrew religion with others around us, warning us to take nothing for granted so that familiarity cannot breed contempt. Our convictions about a holy God are more than a matter of keeping our distance, but there are aspects of truth here which we must retain even if we need to explain them afresh to each generation. After all, if we weren't primitive you couldn't be civilised.

The glory of God

When I speak of the glory of God, I am serious and exuberant at the same time. The picture I see combines brightness and weight. 'To the Israelites the glory of the Lord looked like a consuming fire on top of the mountain' (Ex 24:17). The 'holiness' of God is his unimaginable purity, and the 'glory' of God describes his impact on our lives. We do not see him, but our awareness of his presence often includes something almost visible, almost tangible. We call it his 'glory'. The future may bring us a less fearsome, more personal expression of his glory, but our early insights will not be redundant.

The Lord's instructions to build the Tabernacle included a clear promise: 'Then have them make a sanctuary for me, and I will dwell among them' (Ex 25:8). You may not need a particular place to locate the presence of God but we do. Our word for his dwelling, 'Shekinah', derives from a group of Hebrew words which are associated with living in tents. We focus God's presence in our Tabernacle tent and link his glory to it. Wherever God is, there we talk of his glory which is the impact of his arrival among us. A number of leading ideas surround this concept, especially those of unbelievable brightness and dazzling light. When I climbed Mount Sinai, 'the cloud covered it, and the glory of the Lord settled on Mount Sinai...to the Israelites the glory of the Lord looked like a consuming fire on top of the mountain' (Ex 24:15–17). When I returned to the people with two stone tablets of the Testimony in my hands, many of them took due note of their leader. 'He was not aware that his face was radiant because he had spoken with the Lord' (Ex 34:29). The glory of God leaves an indelible mark on you when you've met him.

This blinding light heralds the coming of the Lord, but its brightness forces us to look away, mystified but not distressed. The clouds, the lightning and the storms reveal the glory of God, and indicate his majestic activity. I saw his glory on the mountain, but no one else spotted anything more than a cloud, which was the beauty of my experience. He overwhelms one man with an awareness which is almost physical, but the same moment either means nothing to others around him or devastates all of them. Although I can't explain that, I accept it as a unique legacy of our Israelite faith.

On another occasion, I was with Aaron while he offered the appropriate sacrifice. Here is the official account of what happened next: 'Moses and Aaron then went into the Tent of Meeting. When they came out, they blessed the people; and the glory of the Lord appeared to all the people. Fire came from the presence of the Lord...and when all the people saw it, they shouted for joy and fell face down' (Lev 9:23–24).

I learned the hard way that we dare not presume on God when he meets us. He offered me anything I wanted, and I took him at his word but received a sharp lesson about praying in harmony with his will. My request was simple enough: 'Now show me your glory' (Ex 33:18). Patient as ever, the Lord made me realise that I did not know what I was asking. I wanted to see his glory, but he answered me in terms of his appearance. 'You cannot see my face, for no one can see me and live' (Ex 33:20). As far as God is concerned, a request to see his glory is a plea to meet him face to

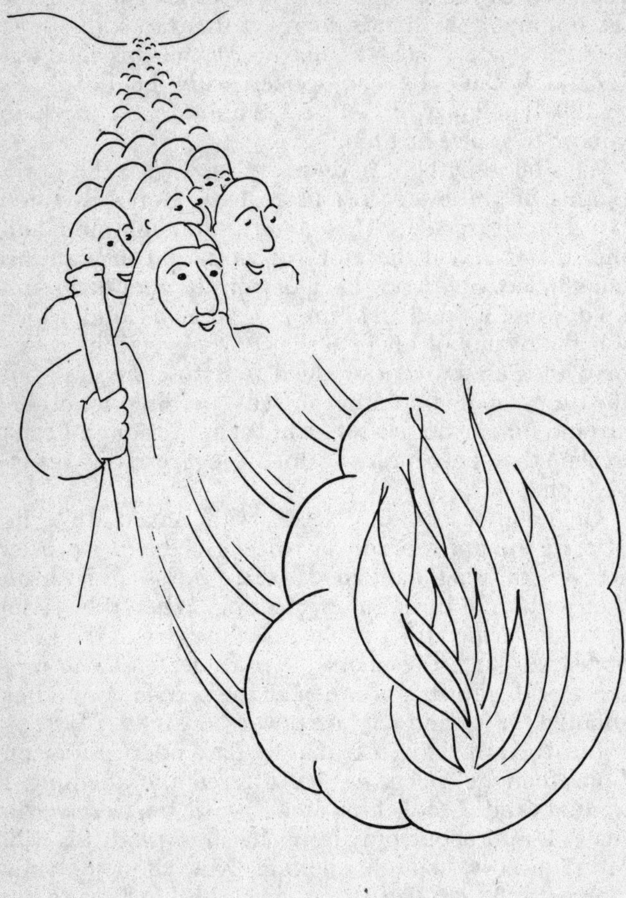

face, and none of us would survive the dire immediacy of that encounter. I have no more wish than you to be burned alive, but I was bitterly disappointed at the time. I felt quiet, emotional and small, which I now know to be a natural response to the glory of God. Think twice before you pray for the Lord's glory.

The fear of God

If mention of the fear of God sends you diving for cover, you've misunderstood the whole idea. If you've ever threatened anyone with the fear of God, especially a child, you'd better watch what you say from now on.

The holiness, the glory and the fear of God belong together as revelation, impact and response. (Yes, it's another three point sermon, but you need a word for 'impact' which begins with 'r'.) When I talk about the fear of God, I'm speaking of a response which includes strong faith and transparent humility. It confesses the Lord as the most important reality in my life by living with an active concern to avoid anything which violates his will. I have experienced the fear of God as a racing of the pulse, a thumping of the heart and a rising of the temperature, but I've also felt tremendously peaceful. Am I making myself clear to you? There is nothing to be afraid of in the fear of the Lord. You may experience this 'fear' in worship, in prayer, in temptation, in social commitment or in human love, and it will be very moving for you when God breaks in with unusual power. It's your response to him which I am labelling 'the fear of God'. We need more time to grasp its full meaning, but we are making progress.

Let me illustrate from an incident which brought the whole of Israel to fear God. 'When the people saw the thunder and lightning and heard the trumpet and saw the mountain in smoke, they trembled with fear...Moses said to the people, "Do not be afraid. God has come to test you, so that the fear of God will be with you to keep you from sinning"...the people remained at a distance, while Moses approached the thick darkness where God was' (Ex 20:18–21). A mature person is someone who copes with a paradox, and we need maturity when we talk about God. The fear of God is a response to him in which we are not afraid. I know it's a bit of a teaser, but I believe it's true, and I suggest you give yourself time to chew on it.

I accept the risk that you will misunderstand what I'm saying about the fear of God, but it's a risk worth taking because I'm exploring a vital part of our relationship with him. It can hold its own if other aspects of truth balance it. It is a necessary response to the Lord. 'And now, O Israel, what does the Lord your God ask of you but to fear the Lord your God, to walk in all his ways, to love him, to serve the Lord your God with all your heart and with all your soul, and to observe the Lord's commands and decrees that I am giving you today for your own good' (Deut 10:12–13).

The religions of our near-eastern world use intricate rites in the hope of placating their implacable gods. We know those rites are unnecessary for us because the core of our faith is God's historic deliverance of our nation from Egypt. Our discoveries of his nature arise out of his activity in the Exodus, and they lead us to wonderful conclusions which make the fear of God as attractive as it is daunting. It is not a dark sky from which we snatch glimpses of sunshine. The Ark of God may terrify us at times, but it also sparks off uninhibited joy with its assurance that he is close to us. The fear of God is a response which realises his majesty and lives in wonder at the power he exerted for our salvation. 'And when the Israelites saw the great power the Lord displayed against the Egyptians, the people feared the Lord and put their trust in him and in Moses his servant' (Ex 14:31).

This fear has one vital partner – 'trust'; I know of no parallel to this partnership in any other religion. The opposite of such fear is a contempt which refuses to honour the Lord. He once said to me, 'How long will these people treat me with contempt? How long will they refuse to believe in me, in spite of all the miraculous signs I have performed among them?' (Num 14:11). He was asking me why the people did not fear him. The fear of the Lord is not a spiritual option for those who are particularly dedicated, it is a right attitude to God to which I have summoned Israel. 'Fear the Lord your God and serve him. Hold fast to him and take your oaths in his name' (Deut 10:20).

The word of God

Our special relationship with God rests solidly on his word. He spoke personally to me and corporately to Israel: 'The Lord said to Moses...' (Ex 12:1; cf 9:13; 10:1; 11:1; 20:1). 'Then the Lord said to Moses, "Tell the Israelites..."' (Ex 14:1; cf 14:15). His word is consistent with his character, expressing his sovereign will which comes to us as a demand on our lives and a promise for the nation. 'He humbled you, causing you to hunger, and then feeding you with manna, which neither you nor your fathers had known, to teach you that man does not live on bread alone but on every word that comes from the mouth of the Lord...observe the commands of the Lord your God, walking in his ways and revering him' (Deut 8:3, 6). God comes out of hiding when he speaks to us, and we are able to know him.

The word of God sustains the life of Israel, and what is true for the nation has also proved true for me. Sons and daughters love to chat with their father and can't accept it if he seems to ignore them. In the same way, the silence of God can feel like an unbearable condemnation, whereas we delight in his word. Sometimes he says hard things, but even they communicate the faithfulness of his continuing concern.

God has met me many times through his word. He has not invited me to a discussion nor offered a deal, but he has summoned me to decisive action. I have been willing, stubborn and reluctant, but he has not adjusted his terms to accommodate my moods. The details he gave us in Egypt for the celebration of Passover did not mince his words. 'Obey these instructions as a lasting ordinance for you and your descendants. When you enter the land that the Lord will give you as he promised, observe this ceremony' (Ex 12:24–25). His words on Mount Sinai were an explicit statement of conditions and promise for a chosen people. 'Now if you obey me fully and keep my covenant, then out of all nations you will be my treasured possession' (Ex 19:5). He blesses those who obey him and curses those who don't. 'See, I am setting before you today a blessing and a curse – the blessing if you obey the commands of the Lord your God that I am giving you today; the curse if you disobey the commands of the Lord your God' (Deut 11:26–28). 'This day I call heaven and earth as witnesses against you that I have set before you life and death, blessings and curses. Now choose life, so that you and your children may live' (Deut 30:19). Clearly, the Lord sets great store by our response to his word, whether of obedience or disobedience.

The God of Israel is one who speaks to his people; I know of no other nation which makes such a claim for its deity. We understand 'the word of God' as a dynamic activity. If God speaks to you, you will not be the same again, which is precisely what he intends. You're wasting your time to pretend you haven't heard him, because he is too experienced in dealing with those who play that game. Our 'deafness' doesn't fool him. I should know, I've tried it often enough. The question is, 'What did you do about it when God spoke to you?'

The guidance of God

Any suggestion that God has a purpose for Israel

implies that he knows what he wants us to do, where he wants us to go and how to make us aware of his will. He chooses times, places and methods, calling us to accept what he is doing; which brings me to the vexed question of guidance.

We know that the Lord works through our circumstances, but how can we be sure that it is his hand which traces the lines we detect? It's a cop out to claim that we only know God's guidance in retrospect. That is a questionable attempt to move from faith into sight which is never possible when we face vital decisions.

I too have despaired: 'Lord, are you there?' 'Lord, what are you doing?' When the people went for me in the drought at Rephidim, I was at a complete loss, trying unsuccessfully to discover God's purpose. Did I miss his guidance? Had he withdrawn from us? Had we lost his message on the way? Was I talking aloud with no serious conviction that anyone was listening? 'What am I to do with these people? They are almost ready to stone me' (Ex 17:4).

We experienced God's guidance through his miraculous provision of food in the aptly named 'desert of Sin'. He rained down bread and meat from heaven when the whole nation was up in arms against Aaron and me. We called it 'bread', but it was more like some of your cereals – endless packets of heaven-sent Frosties. Fortunately, we had no complaints about quality as such – it would have been very awkward to send food back to the manufacturer – though it did get a bit samey. God guided us in those strange days, renewing daily the assurance that we lived within his purpose which took no account of our selfish desires.

The Lord guided us in unusual directions, dispensing with common sense as the essential basis of judgement. He called us to a daring faith which takes risks and proves God. No other form of faith is worthy of the name. How would you convince a hardened sceptic that ours was the best route for an escape from Egypt? 'By day the Lord went ahead of them in a pillar of cloud to guide them on their way and by night in a pillar of fire to give them light, so that they could travel by day or night' (Ex 13:21). Later, the messenger of God who had guided us from the front moved behind us, and the daytime cloud and night-time fire separated us from the pursuing Egyptians (Ex 14:19–20).

If we take the plunge of faith, the Lord won't fail to guide us, but he refuses to do a deal. My commercial instincts have taught me time and again to read the small print before I sign anything, but he has called me to obey him without a contract, and only then have I heard his promise. When I obeyed him by handing in my notice to Jethro, things fell into place for me but I had to act in faith first. When we moved on towards the sea fleeing Pharaoh's pitiless army, we saw a mighty work of God. The moment we accepted today's guidance letting go of yesterday's, the cloud and fire moved on without confusing us. This was not the action of an arbitrary spirit but of a sovereign will.

What Israel has known so far is only a beginning. As we know God better and question his ways, his guidance will become more personal. The quest for the will of God is often painful, causing plenty of rueful heart-searching, but those who act on their faith in a living God are not disappointed.

The living God

The impotence of idols exposes the deception they symbolise, and one day there will be a public showdown (see 1 Kings 18). They are lifeless objects which owe more to naked superstition than to spiritual life, but they still seduce our loyalty and win a big following. We did not carve God out of anything, and we cannot melt him down. He created us, later revealing his name, his character and his will. We need to talk much more of 'the living God', a concept which will quicken our pace and lighten our darkness.

I have discovered the living God, or, more accurately, he has discovered me. He guarded my early, formative years. He watched me flee in terror from Egypt, and he followed me. He stopped me in my tracks with a burning bush. He persuaded me to return to Egypt, issuing careful instructions for our meetings with Pharaoh. He gave us our escape route from Egypt and took us into the sea we preferred to avoid. He shared our wilderness journey whose tortuous conditions provoked his constant reassurance, keeping us from disintegration. He introduced himself many times: 'I am the Lord' (eg Ex 6:2, 6, 29; 7:5; 14:4). He broke through our hasty conclusion that he was absent by the way he took note of our sufferings in Egypt. 'I have indeed seen the misery of my people in Egypt. I have heard them crying out...I am concerned about their suffering...I have come down to rescue them...and to bring them up out of that land...And now the cry of the Israelites has reached me, and I have seen the way the Egyptians are oppressing them' (Ex 3:7–9).

All this brought us to worship. 'And when they heard that the Lord was concerned about them and had seen their misery, they bowed down and worshipped' (Ex 4:31). God did so much for us, repeating his concern for our captivity. 'I have heard the groanings of the Israelites, whom the Egyptians are enslaving, and I have remembered my covenant' (Ex 6:5). He never abandoned us, although the people often accused him. Our history is more than a human story, because the living God breathes through each chapter, and you can't disentangle the statements of faith from the record of history. I dealt with Pharaoh, and two nations shuddered with the conflict, but I came to see what countless believers will experience for themselves: the living God needs no sleep. 'The Lord kept vigil that night' (Ex 12:42).

The mercy of God

I am building a house which I cannot finish; I'm presenting truths which I can't exhaust, and I'm explaining something which can't be understood. That is our dilemma whenever we speak of God, the God who met me and changed my life. Can you imagine how I might have lived if he had not intervened when I was a shepherd, or a fugitive, or a prince, or a baby?

Let me mention one further point about the character of God: his mercy.

My awareness of God's mercy came in prayer when I realised he was pursuing me beyond my stubborn refusal to obey him. When the sin of our nation lies exposed as an irreparable breach of faith, something happens without parallel in any other religion. God does not break his commitment to us, he treats us with mercy. He renews his love to Israel with no obligation on our part except the obligation to believe him and receive his mercy. His desire to forgive freely is his mercy. His steadfast love to those who have no claim on him is his mercy. Future prophets will develop an idea which originates with us: only a God whose heart is beating with mercy forgives sin and creates the fire of new life from the ashes of judgement. 'The Lord is slow to anger, abounding in love and forgiving sin and rebellion...In accordance with your great love, forgive the sin of these people just as you have pardoned them from the time they left Egypt until now' (Num 14:18–19).

We survive by the mercy of God, a mercy which is personal in motive and effect. The next step we must take is to offer that mercy to each other in a human friendship which bears a divine stamp. That is the continuing challenge of our experience of God which I now deliver into your hands.

10
Worship

I hope I can talk freely about worship without you getting all hot under the collar and sending me angry letters of protest – the usual outcome when I risk pen to paper on this provocative subject. Let's see if we can keep cool for once; after all, why waste time falling out about something which should keep us together, not drive us apart? In fact, it ought to be great fun to delve into such a fascinating topic.

Pharaoh accused us of wanting free time for worship because we were lazy. 'They are lazy; that is why they are crying out, "Let us go and sacrifice to our God"' (Ex 5:8). That proves how little he knew about real worship. It is actually a very demanding activity, but too many people treat it as entertainment, reckoning they can rate the performance when it's over.

Our worship is a celebration of everything we believe about God. The historical basis of our faith separates us from the pagan religions which surround us, although we have borrowed some of their ideas and rituals, adapting them to meet our own stringent requirements. The Exodus is now sufficiently central to our worship that it is more difficult to neglect it as the means God used to bring our nation into being than it is to remember it. 'When you have brought the people out of Egypt, you will worship God on this mountain' (Ex 3:12).

I want to outline the main features of our worship so that you can reconsider your own practices and adjust your attitudes, if you're flexible enough.

Hymns

We don't share your ways of labelling singing. Call them 'hymns', 'songs' or 'choruses' if you must, according to your prejudice, but don't forget that many hymns which you've sung happily for years also have choruses, which means that the laugh is on you. The word 'song' is no more than my attempt to avoid the jibes of ignorant people who sneer at 'choruses' and hurt sincere believers in the process. We use the words (lyrics) and music which suit us best. If someone offers the right words, we'll find suitable music, and if there is a good tune, we'll add the words. It doesn't matter whether the song stays in use or not, most people cling so mindlessly to tradition that permanence is no guarantee of quality.

Our experience is that God's mighty works invariably provoke new hymns, and we don't intend to stem the tide. It's pointless to pretend we're in revival if we're not, but we love fresh bursts of praise which keep worship on its toes and stop it stagnating. We won't accept the petty restrictions which you call 'copyright'. They make life difficult for all of us and line the pockets of authors and composers. We are far more concerned to bring worthy offerings to the Lord than we are to commercialise liturgy. Our new songs are not the playthings of people impatient for novelty; they are the wonderful outcome of a mighty salvation. If you allow gifted people to use their creativity for God, you will always have new avenues of worship to explore. Dull people going nowhere refuse the journey which adventurous people gladly accept, and that is particularly true of worship.

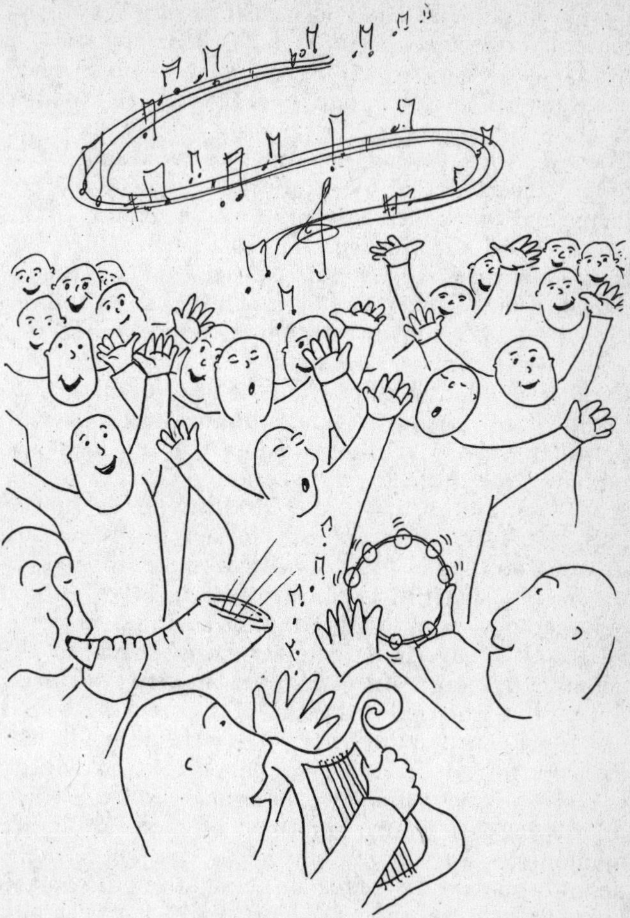

As soon as we crossed the Red Sea, we burst into song. It was an uninhibited and noisy mixture of relief, thankfulness, amazement and triumph. We hadn't packed our hymnbooks when we left Egypt, so we commissioned new verses. They soon poured out (Ex 15:1ff). Whether or not they were meant for posterity was not the point. They were exactly what we wanted – a marvellous blend of bold statement and spontaneous poetry. The context, theme and words of the hymn were a celebration of the Exodus. God had rescued us in a salvation none of us could have achieved for ourselves, and we were determined to praise him: 'The Lord is my strength and my song; he has become my salvation' (Ex 15:2).

We were convinced from the beginning that the Exodus would establish itself as the heart of our corporate life and worship; at no cost must we let it become peripheral. Our worship proclaims that we rooted our faith in God's dramatic intervention to change our history. 'Pharaoh's chariots and his army he has hurled into the sea. The best of Pharaoh's officers are drowned in the sea...They sank like lead in the mighty waters' (Ex 15:4,10). These saving truths have become our theology. 'Your right hand, O Lord, was majestic in power. Your right hand, O Lord, shattered the enemy. In the greatness of your majesty you threw down those who opposed you...Who among the gods is like you, O Lord? Who is like you – majestic in holiness, awesome in glory, working wonders?' (Ex 15:6, 7, 11).

You won't be stunned by the brilliance of every line of the Exodus hymn, but some of them really are memorable. 'In your unfailing love you will lead the people you have redeemed. In your strength you will guide them to your holy dwelling' (Ex 15:13). Our faith is stirred as we offer God's great promises back to him by setting them to music. 'You will bring them in and plant them on the mountain of your inheritance – the place, O Lord, you made for your dwelling, the sanctuary, O Lord, your hands established' (Ex 15:17).

We take the music we find. If you linger in captivity, or panic on the sea-shore, or wander endlessly in the desert, arguments about worship become a luxury you can't afford. Our women provide an important lead whenever the men step aside. They use their own words, blending originality with relevance, and opening up new horizons of praise. 'Then Miriam the prophetess, Aaron's sister, took a tambourine in her hand, and all the women followed her, with tambourines and dancing. Miriam sang to them, "Sing to the Lord, for he is highly exalted. The horse and its rider he has hurled into the sea"' (Ex 15:20–21). Doesn't that sound much more exciting than some of your predictable efforts on a Sabbath morning? (No, I'm not trying to be rude, I just want you to reconsider your worship.) Many women have a natural sense of rhythm, which ensures that their tambourines keep us in time – drums do it even better, especially for large congregations – and the ladies flourish when we men protect them from the cynicism of crushing comment. If you're someone who prefers to clutch a hymnbook with both hands, you'll find tambourines, dancing and exuberant women all rather threatening. But if you follow their example, you'll enter into a freedom which you have secretly longed for, and your days of wistful envy will be over.

The moment you open the door to gifted, if temperamental, people – songwriters, musicians, dancers – you admit an exciting variety of creative contributions which will enrich the whole assembly and increase its enthusiasm.

The Lord told me to invite Bezalel and Oholiab to use their artistic talents so that we could all benefit from them. They introduced wonderful artwork into worship by producing metalwork, banners, tapestries, woodwork, stonework and furnishings. These were not permanent displays, but fresh offerings from people who blessed us as much as they blessed God: 'See I have chosen Bezalel...and I have filled him with the Spirit of God, with skill, ability, and knowledge in all kinds of crafts – to make artistic designs for work in gold, silver and bronze, to cut and set stones, to work in wood, and to engage in all kinds of craftsmanship. Moreover, I have appointed Oholiab...to help him...' (Ex 31:1–6). Isn't that a bigger understanding of what it means to be Spirit-filled than you have, or do I do you an injustice?

This eruption of gifts so moved me that I tried my hand at a worship song (Deut 31:19–32:43). It wasn't as easy as I expected, and I made the mistake of choosing a difficult theme – Israel's rebellious future – but the exercise sharpened my mind and allowed God to speak clearly to me. After all, we don't have to succeed every time we try something new, do we? Do you seriously think I believe that your song writers produce one hit after another? It's the peculiar way some of you talk which amuses me. 'The Lord gave me a song this week.' Did he really? Isn't he a better musician than that? You wrote the song, and you shouldn't blame the Lord who is perfectly happy that you had a good try – and may even have helped you with an overdose of beginner's luck – but a bit wary of your transparent piety which blackmails a congregation by landing a song on them which should never go further than your notebook. As I see it, you're imposing something which should have died before a note was written, but I'm an old man and you don't have to listen to me.

My song put history to music, making it easier to learn. It brought together judgement and warning, and pleaded with Israel to change her ways: 'The Lord will judge his people and have compassion on his servants' (Deut 32:26). My singing voice is nothing to write home about, and for their first performance I decided to read the words rather than sing them. As one tactful reporter put it, 'Moses came with Joshua son of Nun and spoke all the words of this song in the hearing of the people' (Deut 32:44). All my life I had wanted to write a hymn, and only in my old age did I pluck up the courage to have a go. Don't wait as long as I did, but be sensitive how you press the result into the light of day.

Festivals

We already have a full programme of worship planned around the annual calendar. We are great ones for festivals, unashamedly celebrating what the Lord has done for us. We don't hide from our setbacks, but the joyful feasts restore God's perspective to our lives.

The Sabbath (Ex 23:10–13; cf Ex 20:8–11; 31:12–17; Lev 23:3; Deut 5:12–14)

We are learning to use the weekly Sabbath to our advantage. There are dangers in a negative approach to any of God's gifts, and I have little confidence that we shall avoid them. Equally, I expect the pendulum to swing to a reluctance to take any break from the commercial activities for which Hebrews will become famous (see Amos 8:5). I can only repeat God's intention to give us the Sabbath as a day of rest, and we're heading for trouble if we reckon to know better than him. He rested from his creative work, and we need to do the same. 'Six days do your work, but on the seventh do not work, so that your ox and your donkey may rest and the slaves born in your household, and the alien as well, may be refreshed' (Ex 23:12). This is more than a good idea for men, women and animals; it is a gift for the human race, a social necessity.

The Feast of Passover (Ex 23:14–15; cf Lev 23:5–8; Num 28:16–25; Deut 16:1–8)

The Passover feast did not originate with the Exodus, but the Exodus invested it with a completely new meaning relating entirely to our deliverance from

Egypt. We have adopted precise regulations providing for our families to share meat, bread and herbs on the fourteenth evening of the spring month, Abib. You make regular trips to the butcher's to ask for 'lamb chops', 'leg of lamb', 'shoulder of lamb', but we specify the whole animal, sheep or goat. We sprinkle the blood of a young male around our door frames as a sign that we are Israelites because that was how the Lord agreed to 'pass over' Israel when he destroyed the first-born of Egypt. We can't economise by saving today's left-overs for tomorrow's cold meat, which is just as well because I hate cold lamb and Zipporah refuses to hunt out a decent recipe.

We eat everything on the actual night of Passover. Only unleavened bread is allowed for the whole week and some, not unreasonably, call it 'the bread of affliction' (Deut 16:15). I must admit that I prefer proper bread. The bitter herbs eaten with the roast lamb are not choice garden produce, they are wild desert plants which really are bitter, an unmistakable reminder of our plight in Egypt. We eat everything on the same night, and we never slaughter the sacrificial lamb before twilight. That's fine for some people, but if you are one of those infuriating slow eaters who delay the family for hours, please take pity on us and hurry up. We have to sit there until you've finished, and at Passover it doesn't feel like all night, it is all night.

The origins of Passover lie far back in remote history, but we have drawn it into our annual programme of worship. It is more than a graphic reminder of what happened in Egypt, it signifies an act of God which told us we were his chosen people. That conviction is not an abstract idea but a consequence of our spiritual birth. The Lord called me; he called Israel, even in her weakness; he broke Pharaoh's resistance, and he whipped up the winds to divide the sea. Those are the facts of a great story. They explain our confidence that his choice does not rest on arbitrary favouritism but on his will for us to serve him. The Passover will develop in practice, and I stand at the beginning of that process. My great fear is that we shall formalise it by centralising an event intended for family worship which permits circumcised slaves and aliens to share in a unique community celebration. The Passover may face a chequered future, but prophets will rise up to promote a festival which is vital to the continuing life of Israel. (See 2 Kings 23:21ff; 2 Chron 35:1ff; Ezek 45:21ff.)

The Feast of Harvest (Ex 23:16; cf Lev 23:15–22; Num 28:26–31; Deut 16:9–12)

No prizes for guessing that this festival has agricultural origins. In it we celebrate the annual harvest of our firstfruits, the choicest produce we can offer the Lord. Originally, it related to those whose lives were more settled than the nomadic existence of those who celebrated the first Passover. The unleavened bread of the feast points to the new beginning we have experienced in the Exodus, and the leavened bread of the wheat harvest marks the end of frantic pressure, exaggerated by all self-respecting farmers, and a welcome return to normal routine.

This is the only feast which allows us to use yeast for an offering to the Lord: 'Bring two loaves...baked with yeast, as a wave offering of firstfruits to the Lord' (Lev 23:17). Once more, we are adapting an ancient festival to include reference to the Exodus, which greatly increases its joy. 'Remember that you were slaves in Egypt...rejoice before the Lord your God at the place he will choose as a dwelling for his name, you, your sons and daughters, your menservants and maidservants, the Levites in your towns, and the aliens, the fatherless and the widows living among you' (Deut 16:12,11). Some people prefer to call this 'The Feast of Weeks' (Deut 16:10), or 'The Feast of Firstfruits' (Num 28:26). Our celebration begins seven Weeks from the start of the barley harvest, giving us the right time for wheat harvest. 'Count off seven weeks from the time you begin to put the sickle to the standing corn. Then celebrate the Feast of Weeks to the Lord your God' (Deut 16:9).

The Feast of Ingathering (Ex 23:16; cf Lev 23:32–43; Num 29: 12–39; Deut 16:13–17)

The best translation I know for this feast is 'the Feast of Huts', but that's hardly soothing on the ear, and you may decide to stick to 'the Feast of Tabernacles' or 'Booths', which sound better but, strictly speaking, are not accurate.

My own prediction is that this festival more than any other will increase in importance and become very crowded. It is a further legacy from our agricultural origins. At present, we bring an offering from the crops of the fields, the threshing floor and the winepresses. 'On the first day you are to take choice fruit from the trees, and palm fronds, leafy branches and poplars, and rejoice before the Lord your God for seven days' (Lev 23:40). 'Celebrate the Feast of Tabernacles for seven days after you have gathered the produce of your threshing floor and your wine-press' (Deut 16:13). The pressing of the olives and the grapes guarantee a good time for everyone, with the Lord's assured blessing on the festivities. 'Rejoice before the Lord your God' (Lev 23:40).

We have to be careful that things don't get out of hand; you all know what a few drinks can do. I predict that a popular saying will establish itself in Hebrew wisdom: 'The man who has never seen the joy of the night of this feast has never seen real joy in all his life.' (Quoted by R. de Vaux, *Ancient Israel*, Darton, Longman & Todd, p. 496.) Here again, we have transferred the context of the feast to the Exodus. 'Live in booths for seven days. All native born Israelites are to live in booths so that your descendants will know that I made the Israelites live in booths when I brought them out of Egypt. I am the Lord your God' (Lev 32:42–43). This may be a departure from the primary meaning of the feast, but it does link the Exodus to every part of our national life.

The covenant ceremony (Ex 24:1–8)

You may want to question me about our orders of service, especially if you lead worship yourself, and I don't want to give the impression that I'm avoiding this thorny subject. Do we prepare orders of service in advance? Have we agreed to use a fixed liturgy so that some of us can rejoice in familiar words and fine literature while others chafe under restrictive practices?

I have no time for the constant squabbles over forms of worship, but I'm happy to explain our ways of doing things. Our best chance of reaching common ground is to talk more about the content of worship and less about its forms; we Hebrews enjoy the best of both worlds, and I'm sorry if you can't do that with us. On the one hand, we have the jubilant celebrations of our Exodus, which I have already described to you. We offer uninhibited praise with tremendous power, dismissing the fear that cynical critics will accuse us of triumphalism. On the other hand, we value the freedom to be varied, and we have some wonderful liturgies which offer helpful guidelines without imposing the rigidity of straight-jackets.

Our covenant ceremony at the foot of the mountain was a superb example of this latter form, and its renewal provides a stirring act of Hebrew worship with a clear structure within which there is ample freedom. I will set out its main sections, so that you can see what I mean (Ex 24:1ff).

(1) A reading of the Law

'Moses went and told the people all the Lord's words and laws' (Ex 24:3). We do not live by an idea of God or by abstract theological statements which normal people can't understand. We live in the memory of a historical miracle which we relive in worship. Our continuing existence depends on the agreement we made with God at Sinai to be his people living in obedient faith. That agreement is not between two equal parties; it is our recognition of God as Lord, a confession that he has chosen us in the mystery of his love so that we can serve him. 'For you are a people holy to the Lord your God. The Lord your God has chosen you out of all the peoples on the face of the earth to be his people, his treasured possession...you are the fewest of all peoples. But it was because the Lord loved you...that he brought you out with a mighty hand and redeemed you from the land of slavery...' (Deut 7:6–8).

(2) A general confession

I am talking about a confession of God, not of our sin. It is not enough to listen to him; that would make it too easy for us to let the words pass in one ear and out of the other. We have to make a response which commits us to practical obedience. Ours is a corporate confession, an essential concession to our humanity and an exciting proclamation in which we stand together. 'Everything the Lord has said we will do' (Ex 24:3). We are not repeating a boring response of traditional liturgy; we are raising a shout of acclamation which binds us to God.

(3) A sacrifice with blood

'He built an altar at the foot of the mountain and set up twelve stone pillars representing the twelve tribes of Israel. Then he sent young Israelite men and they offered burnt offerings and sacrificed young bulls as fellowship offerings to the Lord' (Ex 24:4–5). The covenant is sealed in blood, and the twelve pillars symbolise the entire nation. I have no idea why sacrifice is so vital in our religion, although I do believe strongly in visible expressions of faith. One day there might be a single, unrepeatable sacrifice which does away with the need for any more, but I am unworthy to contemplate such a deed, let alone offer it.

We often debate the meaning of the blood in sacrifice, and I appreciate that it may seem strange to you that we sprinkled half of the blood over the people and the other half on the altar. I did what God told me to do without fully understanding all I wanted to know, and there is not much more I can tell you.

We are clear that 'the life of a creature is in the blood' (Lev 17:11,14). When the blood is poured out the creature dies, and that blood is a symbol for death. The necessity of sacrifice is the necessity of a death to atone for sin. 'It is the blood that makes atonement for one's life' (Lev 17:11). I am still trying to understand the enormous mystery of sacrificial atonement, but I know the significance of blood shed in sacrifice is of life poured out to death. Somehow, in the hidden purpose of God, that is great news for us, although it's puzzling. That's as far as I can go because I too have unanswered questions. The covenant is sealed in blood and we believe that we shall move slowly but surely to a better understanding of God's sovereign requirements for our worship. In the covenant ceremony, the moment of sacrifice is extremely solemn, and its drama moves us all.

(4) *The final commitment*

'Then he took the Book of the Covenant and read it to the people. They responded, "We will do everything the Lord has said"' (Ex 24:7). It sounds like an unnecessary repetition of the earlier response to the reading of the law (Ex 24:3), but do you retain all you hear at a first reading? We have to hear things several times to absorb them fully, even as we often repeat vows to remind ourselves that we have committed our lives to God. Visual elements are so valuable in worship because we're much better at remembering what we have seen than what we have heard. Our united response at the end of the covenant ceremony binds us together as the assembly leaves for home.

(5) The blessing of assurance

This is vital, and the words linger in the ears of Israel. God has included us, and we are not left out. We may not be worthy, but God has chosen us. 'Moses then took the blood, sprinkled it on the people and said, "This is the blood of the covenant that the Lord has made with you in accordance with all these words"' (Ex 24:8). It is a mighty climax which brings peace and dispels fear. As we grow in this assurance, we demand less attention from personal counsellors besieged by our problems.

When I chiselled out two stone tablets to replace those I had smashed in the shameful episode of the golden calf, we went through a ceremony of covenant renewal. 'Then the Lord said, "I am making a covenant with you. Before all your people I will do wonders never before done in any nation in all the world..."' (Ex 34:10). I gave orders designed to hold Israel in the will of God. They included the destruction of all idols, the exclusive progress of Israel in Canaan, the sexual purity of social and religious life, and the observance of our annual festivals (Ex 34:13–27). It was a glorious moment, and our writers have captured what it meant to me. 'Then the Lord said to Moses, "Write down these words, for in accordance with these words I have made a covenant with you and with Israel"...When Moses came down from Mount Sinai with the two tablets of the Testimony in his hand, he was not aware that his face was radiant because he had spoken with the Lord' (Ex 34:27, 29).

Prayer

I refer here to my personal worship through the work

of prayer which God laid upon me. Ideally, this is a private ministry whose time and integrity, whose fruit and reward are known only to God, and I ask your forgiveness for making it public. However, the testimony of such prayer sometimes has to break out of secrecy so that many can appreciate its importance. God called me to speak – 'Now go; I will help you to speak and will teach you what to say' (Ex 4:12) – and I could not do that unless I prayed. I had to take Israel into my heart so that I felt what God felt for her, otherwise I could not be his representative.

I prayed for the nation because I believed it was the best way available to me of discharging my responsibility of leadership. My plea was for God's mercy instead of his judgement, because I couldn't see how anyone would survive his blistering majesty if he came in anger. I belonged to Israel, and I was unable and unwilling to isolate myself from her guilt. I prayed honestly, recalling God to his promises. In the wake of the golden calf I expected him to be fuming, and he was. 'I have seen these people and they are a stiff-necked people. Now leave me alone so that my anger may burn against them and that I may destroy them' (Ex 32:9–10). I pleaded in the only way I knew, challenging the Lord with my urgent intercession: 'Turn from your fierce anger; relent and do not bring disaster on your people' (Ex 32:12).

My prayer did not mean I was soft on Israel or Aaron; I was hopping mad with all of them, letting fly as soon as I came down the mountain. But they were better off with the fury of Moses than the wrath of God. Abraham's clever prayer for Sodom was my precedent in reducing the size of the righteous remnant, which might be enough to save the nation (Gen 18:16–33). I put my life on the line, if only God would spare Israel: 'But now, please forgive their sin, but if not, then blot me out of the book you have written' (Ex 32:32). You can't go further than that in praying for others, but no one will be a valid substitute when God comes in judgement; only he can conceive what that means and act on it.

Our attitude to worship says so much about us. Worship is a dynamic exercise, a strenuous activity more than a dose of comfort, pulling the whole of life into its orbit. If we truly honour God, we treat worship as an involvement in life more than an escape from it. We avoid the tragedy of a futile offering which God rejects for its blind irrelevance. He wants to open our eyes, helping us to welcome what we see and to rejoice in what he does.

We look back to the Exodus, we relive its drama, and we expect further great works of God. In other words, our worship focuses on past, present and future in one great event. Let's ensure that this is as much our regular experience as our constant ideal, so that we never achieve less than God has planned for us. Then no one will call you lazy when you want time to bring the Lord an offering which is worthy of him and a joy for you (see Ex 5:8).

Oh, by the way, thank you for reading on and not blowing up. Is that the first time you've sat through a discussion of worship and not lost your cool? If so, you've done well, and lots of people in your congregation are heaving huge sighs of relief. Bring on the tambourines, but leave the drums for another week; you can't afford to push your luck too far.

11

The Ten Commandments

'Moses was there with the Lord forty days and forty nights without eating bread or drinking water. And he wrote on the tablets the words of the covenant, the Ten Commandments' (Ex 34:28).

You've heard of the Ten Commandments, and you may have used them as a weapon to brandish moral indignation at those who incur your prim disapproval. I can hear you saying it, and it does sound remarkably smug: 'Of course, I still believe in the Ten Commandments.' Let me ask you: How many of the commandments can you list? Do you know where to find them? When did you last read them? (see Ex 20:1–17; Deut 5:6–21).

If we investigate the Ten Commandments, we discover that they form a code which expresses a positive and vital response to God. They are not meant to be good ideas which never see the light of day. And they are certainly not dead letters.

On the mountain, God gave me laws of warning and promise. Their validity extends far beyond our national borders, but our first duty is to apply them to Israel as his gift to a chosen nation. 'The Lord our God made a covenant with us at Horeb. It was not with our fathers that the Lord made this covenant, but with us, with all of us who are alive here today...These are the commandments the Lord proclaimed in a loud voice to your whole assembly there on the mountain from out of the fire, the cloud, and the deep darkness; and he added nothing more. Then he wrote them on two stone tablets and gave them to me' (Deut 5:2, 22).

The Ten Commandments summarise God's will for Israel. They have a precise historical setting and you should not pull them out of that context as if they are timeless truths which hang easily on any moral peg. You can argue as much as you like that they are too difficult to fulfil, but their bruising impact on you actually highlights your preference to do your own thing. These commandments concede nothing to our eagerness for disobedience and, although they focus attention on our behaviour, their greater concern is to probe deeper than outward performance to claim our full allegiance. We shall not exhaust their scope until a unique teacher expounds their unlimited demands on the way we think as well as the way we behave (see Mt 5:17–48).

When God gave the commandments, he spoke directly to Israel. On many previous occasions, when he had something to put to his chosen people, he used me as a mediator. 'Then the Lord said to Moses, "Tell the Israelites this..."' (Ex 20:22). 'The Lord said to Moses, "Speak to Aaron and his sons and to all the Israelites and say to them: 'This is what the Lord has commanded...'"' (Lev 17:1). 'These are the commands, decrees and laws the Lord your God directed me to teach you to observe in the land you are crossing the Jordan to possess...' (Deut 6:1). This time it was different; he took a direct route to the people, dispensing with the services of mediator and priests. 'And God spoke all these words' (Ex 20:1). 'The Lord spoke to you face to face out of the fire on the mountain' (Deut 5:4). This direct communication took Israel by surprise, but I know everyone was excited that the Lord had spoken personally to them. They enjoyed the rare privilege of their generation, and this sharpened their minds to understand what God was telling them.

I have accepted the fact that I shall not lead Israel into Canaan; no such happy ending to the story for me. God called me to serve him, which I'm still doing, but he won't need me for much longer. I have come to terms with the disappointment of leaving the action when it's most attractive to stay in it, and God's decision is the same as the umpire's – final. I'm not one of the Patriarchs, and you must not venerate my tomb or preserve Mosaic relics which will tempt people to value, even to idolise, impotent objects. Joseph lumbered us with a few problems, and I don't intend to dish out similar difficulties to those who follow me. If only people would check with their friends before indulging themselves in a will containing extremely inconvenient instructions (see Ex 13:19; Deut 34:6). I'm already a bit of a relic, and when my time is up I shall go quietly. Please transfer your loyalty to Joshua, and let me go.

If I maintain an active influence after my death, may it not cause you to reverence me but free you to obey God. I am laying foundations for Israel rather than presenting final decrees, which makes it important that you keep your memory of my life in perspective. Inevitably, time will adapt my teaching, and I don't want you to isolate the things I have said for special authority. There is no book called, 'The Sayings of Moses', and if anyone suggests otherwise, he's a fraud. A prophet speaks first to his own day, and that is what I have done. If my words remain relevant to later generations, all well and good; it will save God the bother of calling new prophets, but that is his concern and my impression is that he plans to use many men after me. 'The Lord your God will raise up for you a prophet like me from among your own brothers. You must listen to him' (Deut 18:15). I stand at the beginning of a long line of those who speak for God. It will be a distinguished line, but it will suffer in its cause of courageous service.

Whatever you do, don't forget that the Ten Commandments are a vivid summary of the law which assumes our deliverance from Egypt. Through that rescue, God staked his claim to Israel. In the law he gave on Mount Sinai he set out an appropriate way of life for the people he wanted to stimulate into grateful living. On the mountain, he forged a covenant with us, teaching us what he expects from people he has rescued with no obligation on his part and loved with no prior commitment on our part.

I'm always reminding Israel not to reduce the celebration of the Exodus. No, it's not a record stuck in a groove, it's a crucial restatement of the basis of our faith. 'Celebrate the Feast of Unleavened Bread, because it was on this very day that I brought your divisions out of Egypt' (Ex 12:17). 'Celebrate the Passover of the Lord your God...Do not eat it with bread made with yeast, but for seven days eat unleavened bread...because you left Egypt in haste, so that all the days of your life you may remember the time of your departure from Egypt' (Deut 16:1, 3).

The Ten Commandments emphasise the fact that our laws call for a response to God's initiative. He acted first, saving us because of his love for us. Our response is to live worthily of him. The commandments describe the nature of that life. They do not spoil our enjoyment or restrict our freedom; they define the best way of honouring God and of behaving like people who are special to him. As a king or queen urges their son who is a prince, 'Remember who you are,' so God urges us in the Ten Commandments 'Remember who you are.' He has planned our future in Canaan, and our attitude to the commandments signals to him whether or not we're committed to his will. He brought us out of Egypt, and we belong to him through an exodus salvation. The Ten Commandments are the trademark of

God's covenant people, integrating religious faith into national life and emptying the word 'secular' from our Hebrew vocabulary.

It is this conscious relation of our law to the will of God which distinguishes it from the laws of other nations. It doesn't matter whether you think of ritual regulations or social demands, God's sanctions extend to both. If you disobey the law, you disobey God. I know something about the Babylonian Code of Hammurabi because of the widespread reputation it enjoys. It speaks of the will of the Babylonian god Shamash, but only in the opening and closing formulae of the code. By doing this, the Babylonians add religious sanctions to a process which is entirely secular, even pagan. That is light years away from the significance we give the Lord when we announce our law. We don't separate religion, law and morality, and neither will you if you are serious about submitting your community life to God.

I was the mediator of God's law to Israel, but I only delivered what he had entrusted to me. Our near-eastern world has no parallel for this ordering of national life through a spiritual encounter with God. As I concentrated on him in prayer and worship, I understood his demand on Israel. The Ten Commandments are a brilliant summary of many requirements detailed in our sacred writings. Some of them may take hundreds of years to reach their final form, but they will last for ever to nourish the faithful and keep the scholars out of mischief – two great blessings for all of us.

Our laws have clear goals, and I will mention some of the more important of them. If you're still sermon hunting, have your notebooks ready for four headings and four 'p's.

To proclaim faith

'I am the Lord your God who brought you out of

Egypt, out of the land of slavery' (Ex 20:2). This is not an introduction to the real meat, it is an essential statement of the context for all that follows. The commandments are God-centred laws for God-centred people. They inspire us to worship and offer practical teaching. They are a proclamation of our Hebrew faith, and a guide as to how to live it out.

Our moral concern flows from our spiritual life. The Ten Commandments have their source in God's revelation to us on Mount Sinai. I had no idea that my face was radiant after I'd been up the mountain to fetch replacement stone tablets, but I presume I was reflecting the shattering impact of God's presence (Ex 34:29).

Our commandments have a religious foundation which the early commands make explicit by prohibiting gods, idols and all abuse of the Lord's name and by establishing the Sabbath as a day which is holy 'to the Lord your God' (Ex 20:10). The ban on images has led some to conclude that I'm referring to pagan idols, but my primary aim is to reject images of God. His furious reaction to the golden calf suggests that I'm right, and it's my conviction that a negative statement of the commandments elsewhere supports this view. 'Cursed is the man who carves an image or casts an idol – a thing detestable to the Lord, the work of the craftsman's hands – and sets it up in secret. Then all the people shall say, "Amen"' (Deut 27:15).

We expand this ban on images and idols in our preaching of the commandments. 'You saw no form of any kind the day the Lord spoke to you at Horeb out of the fire. Therefore watch yourselves very carefully, so that you do not become corrupt and make for yourselves an idol, an image of any shape' (Deut 4:15ff). Idols trespass on territory which God has reserved for himself, seducing us from our essential spirituality which is obedience to his word. We think other people are godless because they have idols; they think we are godless because we have none! But it would be so easy in these superstitious times to worship objects innocently planned as symbols of God but turning out to be pagan rivals. That's why I reacted as I did to the golden calf, and history will prove me right, even as God's anger at the time justified mine (Ex 32:19–22, 10).

You will not be surprised that we have a commandment forbidding all abuse of God's name. 'You shall not misuse the name of the Lord your God, for the Lord will not hold anyone guiltless who misuses his name' (Ex 20:7). We need to watch what we say. Haven't you noticed how quickly conversation degenerates when a group of men come together? One tries to outdo the others in pushing language towards obscenity, and it's not long before they drag in the name of the Lord, with little idea that their talk is dangerous.

The name of God is more powerful than most people realise, and we should think twice before we use it. When I returned to Egypt to ask Pharaoh's permission to lead the Israelites to freedom, I insisted on knowing the name of the God in whose authority I went (Ex 3:13). His name is too important to ignore and too awesome to abuse. Among our commandments is one which forbids the use of God's name to authorise an oath intending evil against another person. The meaning of the commandment is not immediately obvious, but that is how we interpret it at present. 'Do not swear falsely by my name and so profane the name of your God. I am the Lord' (Lev 19:12). One day the new teacher I have already foretold will blend absolute authority with unique simplicity. He will call us to a scrupulous honesty which removes the need for oaths to guarantee our integrity. Our 'yes' and 'no' will mean what they say. (See Mt 5:33–37.)

To promote community

We are a nation coming to birth and forming its identity. We derive our purpose from God's will because we exist for him, but we are tempted all the time to please ourselves. The Ten Commandments unfold his concern for our social morality, and we have learned to recognise the signs of a healthy community and of one in decay. The commandments direct our attempt to build a strong community which upholds God's standards with active enthusiasm. Most people are thoroughly reasonable alone, but many of us are terrors in a group, and we need help to develop into well-integrated adults capable of mature relationships.

Our Sabbath is for God, but one day's break each week is important for us, and we ignore it at our peril. He has called us to regard one day in seven as 'holy', a day reserved for him. Its intention is positive, not negative. 'Remember the Sabbath day by keeping it holy' (Ex 20:8). The list of Sabbath prohibitions does not exist to destroy our fun but to promote the value of a special day each week (Ex 20:9–11). It's more than a matter of doing no work and having a rest, and it's more than a list of restrictions which irritate us but do not turn us to God. We miss the joy of a willing offering to the Lord when we violate his day, and that is a more serious deprivation than we realise.

I view the Sabbath as God's wonderful gift to the nation, and believe we must spend more energy in making it work well than in finding a way round its requirements. It is both short-sighted and arrogant to imagine that we can exclude ourselves from the essential rhythm of work and rest which the Sabbath spells out. We must also provide adequate safeguards for those who are too weak to protect themselves. Some people assess the quality of a community by the way it treats its animals. The scope of one day's rest each week includes our animals who, like human beings, give far better service if they have regular breaks.

The Sabbath is a social necessity and an expression of our obedience to God. It makes good sense for humanitarian and theological reasons. 'For in six days the Lord made the heavens and the earth, the sea, and all that is in them, but he rested on the seventh day. Therefore the Lord blessed the Sabbath day and made it holy' (Ex 20:11).

We remember our bitter suffering when the remorseless Egyptians ground us into the dust with never a hint of a day off, still less a holiday. Now that we have some control of our own fate, we must protect the entire community from a similar predicament. Good masters need no telling, but the Sabbath command covers us all. Careful regulations elsewhere forbid us to treat our servants as less than human, and we must not regard them as our property. 'If you buy a Hebrew servant, he is to serve you for six years. But in the seventh year, he shall go free, without paying anything. If he comes alone, he is to go free alone, but if he has a wife when he comes, she is to go with him' (Ex 21:2–3).

To prevent evil

Our Ten Commandments contain detailed prohibitions: 'You shall not murder'; 'You shall not commit adultery'; 'You shall not steal'; 'You shall not covet your neighbour's house' (Ex 20:13–17). They are neither complicated to recite nor difficult to understand. You can't argue away their intentions, and you don't need advanced knowledge of Hebrew or meticulous study of commentaries to tease out their meaning; just don't do it.

The Ten Commandments keep the word 'no' in our moral vocabulary as a vital safeguard for community life. The trouble is that when you tell people not to do something, it becomes the one thing they most want to do. But the commands stand, because some things are unacceptable at any price, and that's all there is to it. No 'ifs' and 'buts' allow us to escape the authority of God's unambiguous word.

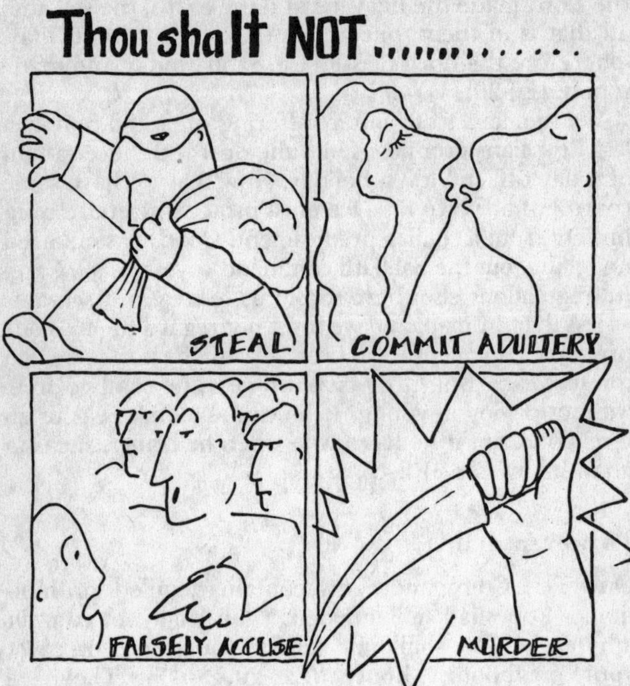
Thou shalt NOT ....
STEAL
COMMIT ADULTERY
FALSELY ACCUSE
MURDER

We can't obliterate evil, but we can reduce its damage by establishing clear limits to the freedom one person has to impose himself on another. We must hang on to the word 'no', while recognising that a society greedy for instant satisfaction rears up at the slightest sniff of personal restriction. People brought up to expect what they want and to get what they expect are only too willing to climb on the backs of victims if that's what it takes to achieve their own ends. We must make that as hard as possible if we want to preserve a caring community in Israel. Those who are greedy for money steal for it; those who bear vicious grudges murder to avenge their hatred; those who burn with envy covet what does not belong to them; those who throb with lust satisfy themselves with no scruples about adultery; and those whose minds are set on quick advantage lie shamelessly to secure it.

The prohibitions of our Ten Commandments oppose evil but they also prepare the ground for positive alternatives. One thing we must do is to ensure that honest witness thrives in Israel. 'One witness is not enough to convict a man accused of any crime or offence he may have committed. A matter must be established by the testimony of two or three witnesses' (Deut 19:15). Lying witness inflicts terrible injustice on individuals and ruins the trust essential for a society built to last. The future will produce disturbing examples of false witness, and we do well even now to regard this as a matter of grave concern in a nation which speaks of God as much as we do (see 1 Kings 21:10–14; Mk 14:47; Acts 6:13). The ninth commandment takes very few words to put it plainly: 'You shall not give false testimony against your neighbour' (Ex 20:16).

We believe in moral absolutes. Some things are wrong and some are right, and you can't change the rules or move the posts to suit yourself. However important you think you are, you have no right to plan something which hurts another person, even if the likely benefits are particularly compelling. I've told you how seriously we view liars, and we're equally severe with adulterers. Their pleasure does not legitimise their rape of marriage, not for one minute, and too many people suffer in the process. It's too easy for a couple to plead, 'But we understand each other,' as if that justifies their treachery. Joseph recoiled in horror from the sexual advances of Potiphar's wife, despite the obvious attraction of her offer. He would have sinned against God as well as Potiphar if he had yielded to the wretched woman. 'How then could I do such a wicked thing and sin against God?' (Gen 39:9). Too often we use our principles to act piously when we're not under temptation and to criticise the behaviour of other people, but we keep them only as long as it suits us to do so. The Ten Commandments are for 'me' and for 'you'; they're not just for 'him', 'her', and 'them'.

In additional laws, we limit revenge and punishment, trying to break the vicious circles which quickly perpetuate suffering by prolonging evil and refusing mercy. We do mention the death penalty, but here in the Ten Commandments we make no reference to it.

If we want to develop these commandments, we'll have to delve deeper into the human heart. Why do we commit murder, adultery, theft? Why do we lie? What is this incurable disease we call 'jealousy', and why does it consume us? Only God changes our hearts, only he calms our inner storms and persuades us to be different. But our laws protect the community, claiming divine authority and binding each individual, irrespective of status or wealth. You can't do what you like, whatever your family, your position or your money, and you'll have to reckon with the God of the Ten Commandments if you try. Your affluence won't protect you and your poverty won't excuse you.

To preserve the family

The Ten Commandments promote strong family life,

although we too have problem families. God's will is that we should live as families in which husbands and wives, fathers and mothers, share an exclusive mutual commitment. This allegiance includes the promise of sexual faithfulness which separates one man and woman to each other from the moment of their marriage. 'You shall not commit adultery' (Ex 20:14) is a command to honour family life. Other laws which condemn fornication as a sexual activity abhorrent to God affect those who may not be married, but adultery is a particular violation of marriage with which few wronged partners can cope. Married people cannot guarantee their own immunity from attraction to other members of the opposite sex – active chemistry is no respecter of persons – but they can make an unconditional promise to be faithful to their partners. Adultery betrays that promise, exposing the adulterer as a liar whose word means nothing.

If we want to preserve the family, we must fight for everything which helps us to succeed, and the Ten Commandments contain vital material for our benefit. A single person may feel that this emphasis on family life is unhelpful or even hurtful. That's too big a subject to tackle now, but surely we all benefit from a community which strongly supports the values I'm promoting here? We also need a big enough understanding of family life to create in each person a reassuring confidence of inclusion rather than exclusion.

In the ebb and flow of moral values, we need standards which don't change, boundaries which we can't alter. One age welcomes the call to 'honour your father and your mother, so that you may live long in the land your God is giving you' (Ex 20:12). A less stable generation is irritated as the pendulum swings in favour of self-assertion free from the twin curbs of authority and discipline.

The Ten Commandments declare the mind of God for the family. The way we honour our parents changes as we grow older and exercise a more independent judgement, but that only alters the form honour takes, it doesn't rule it out. Wise parents release their children into a maturity which welcomes parental counsel when it offers warm encouragement and stifles unwanted criticism. The marriage of a son or daughter further adjusts the responsibility to parents, as a new wife or husband and consequent children assume greater priority in the family pecking order. But the call to honour parents stands because they never lose their major role in the lives of children for whom they are irreplaceable. God takes a dim view of those who violate his commandment, although he does have wise advice for parents who make life as difficult for themselves as for their adult children by demanding as rights those things which love must be free to offer as a gift or to withhold.

I have a vision of the fun families can share in working out God's will, especially when no one makes selfish demands and each person freely gives grateful love, parents as much as children, children as much as parents. This quickly develops into mutual honour which is neither stuffy nor distant.

We do have some stern warnings: 'Cursed is the man who dishonours his father or his mother. Then all the people shall say, "Amen"' (Deut 27:16). We know that all members of the family need the careful teaching given in the expansion of our law. 'These commandments that I give you today are to be upon your hearts. Impress them on your children. Talk about them when you sit at home and when you walk along the road, when you lie down and when you get up' (Deut 6:6–7). That sounds a great idea, and it is, but if you do it without a laugh, you've missed the point. Have you tried imposing a Sunday school lesson on children while you're walking down the road? Most of the kids I know would rather kick stones.

In these commandments we fix the posts, and further teaching will nail in the fencing. We want to create an environment where father and mother find mutual security, where children live in the active assurance of their parents' love for each other and where they honour both parents for the life they have received and the example they try to follow.

The Ten Commandments are the tip of the Hebrew iceberg. There's much more teaching to come. That teaching will expand on the themes of the commandments without destroying their impact. Whenever we translate these vital principles into practical obedience to God, we show him how much we value our salvation and we demonstrate the unique force of our national faith.

12

The Mountain and the Desert

I spent a great deal of time travelling between the mountain and the desert. If I was not pressing on with our wilderness journey, I was climbing a mountain, staying at the top or making my way down. There is a world of difference between these two places, and they have become symbols to me; the one of wonderful experiences, the other of disappointments in my life which has been full of ups and downs. This final chapter describes some of these high and low points in terms of the mountain and the desert.

The mountain top

I've no idea how many times I went up mountains. I usually spent a while at the top. Only novice mountaineers hurry down, having notched up another peak. But when I climb high, I'm not driven by ambition or energised by a consuming hobby. I hit the mountain only when God summons me to meet him.

(1) The place of privilege
I always waited for God to invite me to the mountain top, because I could not manipulate such an experience. There is no obvious reason why he chose me for

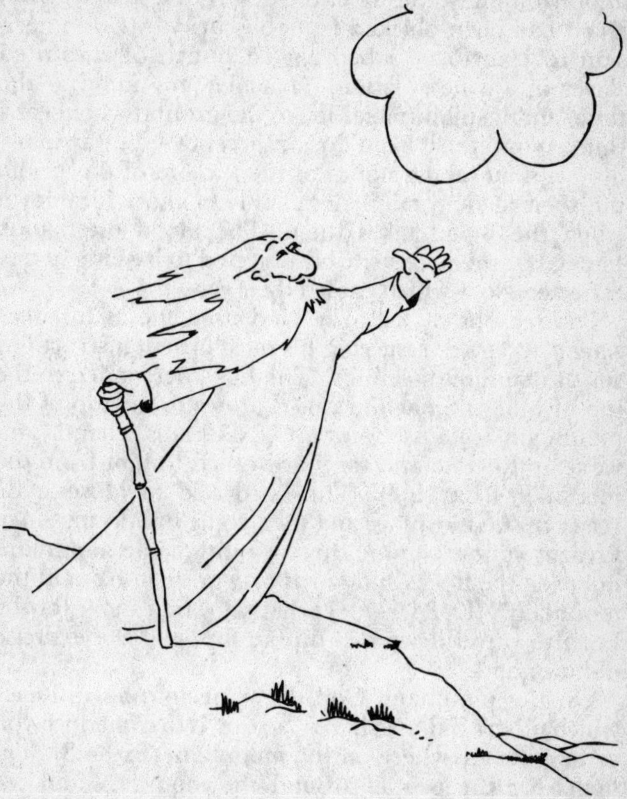

this incredible privilege, a privilege which often terrified me. I was a fugitive murderer, sentenced by my adoptive family, hiding in the desert of a strange land. But I had been plucked from obscurity by God's decision to transform a bedraggled bunch of dispirited slaves into a new nation. That blew my mind at the time, and it still humbles me to the ground whenever I think about it. All I can do is to accept God's way in my life, without taking notice of the acclaim of those who put their leader on a pedestal only to knock him down when the mood takes them. The mood often took Israel, but the people rarely objected to basking in any reflected glory which passed their way.

For reasons of his own, God used me as his messenger to Israel, reserving his most urgent instructions for our summit meetings. 'The Lord descended to the top of Mount Sinai and called Moses to the top of the mountain. So Moses went up' (Ex 19:20). 'Then Moses went up to God, and the Lord called to him from the mountain' (Ex 19:3). 'The Lord said to Moses..."Be ready in the morning, and then come up Mount Sinai. Present yourself to me there on top of the mountain; not even the flocks and herds may graze in front of the mountain"' (Ex 34:1–3). Perhaps it wasn't so far for the Lord to travel if we met on the top, and the exercise did me good.

On the mountain, God drew me into an intimacy which others did not share. 'No one is to come with you or be seen anywhere on the mountain' (Ex 34:3). 'Put limits for the people around the mountain and tell them, "Be careful that you do not go up the mountain or touch the foot of it. Whoever touches the mountain shall be put to death"' (Ex 19:12). We have lived in an unusually formative time when God has revealed special aspects of his holiness and glory. He has disclosed their meaning in pictures of distance over against nearness and intimate presence in tension with unapproachable brightness. My freedom to draw near to him, coupled with his insistence on the people keeping their distance, have been visual aids to the truths of a holy and glorious God. I have met him in the name of Israel, and he has sent me back to Israel in his name, never allowing me to be anything more than his servant. Most of the time I climbed alone, unless the Lord summoned Aaron to accompany me, but I was not lonely. Whenever God appeared in majestic glory, I longed to stay with him for ever. His presence ruled out the possibility of loneliness, providing an assurance which was my enduring strength. I was lost in gratitude and wonder.

I don't think I've seen the last of God's glory on the mountain top. A strange conviction, even a sixth sense, suggests I may know more of his transforming glory. The feeling is vague and tentative, but take good note of my hint (cf Mk 9:2–8). Your mountain experience with God may not come on the physical heights, but it will be a spiritual peak, a time when wonderful things happen for you. You will hear him speak more clearly than ever before. His presence will move you to greater faith from which you serve him more effectively. You will see things to which you were previously blind, and they will cause you to marvel that unseen truths are so vivid. This will make you willing to obey God because his glory has offered you a glimpse of the new dimension we shall experience as 'eternity'. Don't ask to stay for ever on the mountain, but let it change your desert. The mountain stands high over the desert, bringing to it a new perspective so that huge wilderness obstacles shrink to manageable proportions, but only the mountain can help you to see that. The view from the top is God's way of preparing you to do things his way on the low ground.

(2) The place of temptation

There is a temptation which is peculiar to the mountain-top. The most wonderful times of closeness to God can be spoilt by suffering damage which seems at the time to be irreparable. The mountain-top experience tempts us to rush in with hasty ideas, jarring words and uninspired suggestions, but the Lord resists these because he wants us to be quiet and listen. It may be no more than our instinctive enthusiasm, but we are presuming on God when he has neither spoken nor led the way. We are tempted to linger, wanting to be with him to escape a world of pressure and suffering, but we miss the point of the mountain when we try to stay there. He calls us to the top, but sends us back to live where the air is normal.

When we languished in Egypt, God saw it all from his height, he took note of our suffering, he heard our cries and came to our rescue (Ex 3:7–9). We were helpless, discouraged, oppressed, and poor, but he sided with us. As soon as we had control of our own affairs, he reminded us to respect our servants, to integrate aliens and to care for the bereaved (Ex 20:8; 21:2; 22:22; 23:9; Deut 10:18–19). We cannot expect to stay on the mountain aloof from those whose cries reach the Lord as our cries reach him. We have to come down as he came down. One day he will come to us more completely than we can yet imagine, but that day is still a remote dream.

(3) The place of challenge

God spoke powerfully while I was on top of the mountain, but the working out of his word lay back in the desert where people lived and struggled, and spiritual powers clashed. The challenge came on the high ground, but it drove me to return to Israel, often reluctantly, for I knew what awaited my arrival.

The air on top is bracing. You feel full of life, even at my age. You have climbed well, your muscles are loose, and your legs are warm. Others may be tired and you may be sore tomorrow, but today you're exhilarated. The challenge of the mountain is the challenge to fulfil

God's purpose. It is the challenge to live with the view from the top, to spend time in the quiet, to catch the direction of the wind, and to return a different person.

Take your mountain-top experience with you; don't leave it to evaporate in the wistful memory of a privileged hour. The summit must spill over to the crowded plains where the majority spend their lives. The height will remain with you as a sign of hope, beckoning you to a new view of the desert and a stronger awareness of its potential. God has drawn you into his presence, allowing you a view which others may never see. You will need infinite patience and sensitive wisdom to share your insights, and sometimes your impatience will boil over in frustration as you forget that you have enjoyed a rare privilege which God gave you for the benefit of many people, not for your private indulgence.

The desert

'Then Moses led Israel from the Red Sea and they went into the desert of Shur...The Israelites ate manna for forty years, until they came to a land that was settled; they ate manna until they reached the border of Canaan' (Ex 16:1, 35). My account of forty desert years may be patchy, but I've checked its accuracy as far as I can. We lived in the desert with a diminishing hold on the promises of God. My occasional trips up the mountain broke the grip of the wilderness and renewed my commitment to the future. The whole experience taught me the spiritual significance of a desert.

(1) The place of temptation

The desert temptation is not the same as that of the mountain, but it is no less real. One day you will have a record of desert temptation more stark and more dramatic than mine, but until then, I will point the way for you (cf Mt 4:1–11).

We demand scapegoats for our failures, and we blame our downfalls, especially those of our children, on to 'bad company', 'difficult circumstances', and 'deprived conditions'; but the desert shows where the problem really lies. Our creation story proves that we first sinned in a perfect environment (Gen 3:1-7). In the desert I battled not with my circumstances but with my ambition, my desires, my anger and my reluctance to obey God. I fled to the desert of Midian after I murdered the Egyptian bully (Ex 2:15). There are several possible excuses for my crime, but the fact is that it was an act of blind rage. I was often alone in the desert, but that didn't keep me from temptation. Is it any different for you?

The truth about me is the truth about Israel – we were tempted in the desert. Hunger and thirst lured us to spiritual rebellion. We had terrible problems finding water, but vital spiritual issues were at stake which put our journey in serious jeopardy. We grumbled in the desert of Sin: 'If only we had died by the Lord's hand in Egypt' (Ex 16:3). No, this was not the worst catastrophe since time began, it was not the most awful disaster in living memory; we were thirsty. There, in the desert, God fed us and our daily menu did not change for forty years. 'The Israelites ate manna for forty years, until they came to a land that was settled' (Ex 16:35).

The word 'manna' is not an exotic name dreamed up by advertisers flooding the market with a new product. It is Hebrew for 'what is it?' When the food arrived on the first morning, 'thin flakes like frost on the ground' (Ex 16:14), the grumblers pondered the unexpected carpet with suspicion. They reacted like ungrateful children facing a plate of food they refuse to taste but are sure they dislike: 'What's that?' Their blatant disgust intended to depress the heavenly chef, but I stood in his place, offering an explanation so calm that every harassed mother will envy my restraint: 'It is the bread the Lord has given you to eat' (Ex 16:15). No prizes for guessing what I really wanted to say.

The desert had sapped our will to obey God, and my position of leadership suddenly became precarious. I gave firm orders, repeating what God had told me, and a pattern of response began to emerge: 'However some of them paid no attention to Moses; they kept part of it until morning, but it was full of maggots and began to smell. So Moses was angry with them' (Ex 16:20). In the desert, we strayed further into disobedience as furtive rebels crept out on the Sabbath to gather forbidden supplies, only to find that they were caught empty-handed and God had the laugh on them. '"Six days are you to gather it, but on the seventh day, the Sabbath, there will not be any." Nevertheless, some of the people went out on the seventh day to gather it, but they found none' (Ex 16:26–27). Fancy getting up early on the Sabbath and finding it's wasted effort!

(2) The place of preparation

I wish I had been more aware of spiritual power in the desert, but I knew God was preparing me for something ahead. In the same way, he kept us there for forty years until he decided we were ready for Canaan, which is where we now stand. We have come to the brink of our dreams, and once I have died, the nation will move in. It's very difficult to feel wanted in such circumstances, and if anyone realises the truth, he'll press something potent into my goat's milk cheese or stir it into my desert yoghurt to hasten my departure.

My view of the desert as a place of preparation prompts me to ask questions as soon as I realise God is at work. If I can put the right questions, the desert won't be wasted. 'Lord, I know you are preparing me for something, that's why this desert experience is with me. All I'm asking is that you explain what's happening.' The time we spend moaning would be so different if we reckoned with the way God works when he takes his people into the wilderness.

On two occasions I fasted for forty days and nights, both of them on the mountain. In these periods of intense spiritual activity, the desert accompanied me to the heights. 'When I went up the mountain to receive the tablets of stone, the tablets of the covenant that the Lord has made with you, I stayed on the mountain forty days and forty nights; I ate no bread and drank no water' (Deut 9:9). 'Then once again I fell prostrate before the Lord for forty days and forty nights; I ate no bread and drank no water, because of all the sin you had committed' (Deut 9:18–19 cf Ex 34:28). I went through a desert experience on the mountain when I drew near to God seeking to know his will. My fasting is a part of my spiritual life. It has no value apart from this except, possibly, a temporary reduction in weight. I believe it links into repentance, prayer and spiritual integrity to secure breakthroughs with God which I can explain but not prove.

We were wandering in the desert, but God was preparing us. It was not an aimless journey, despite our nagging doubts, and he never withdrew his promises. 'If you listen carefully to the voice of the Lord your God and do what is right in his eyes, if you pay attention to his commands and keep all his decrees, I will not bring on you any of the diseases I brought on the Egyptians, for I am the Lord who heals you' (Ex 15:26). These assurances brought us to Elim, the place of water and palm trees. 'Then they came to Elim, where there were twelve springs and seventy palm trees, and they camped there near the water' (Ex 15:27). The more we believed God's promises, the more we were ready to face scarcity, to notice blessing and to trust him. 'Worship the Lord your God, and his blessing will be on your food and water' (Ex 23:25).

(3) The place of quiet

God leads you into the desert to remove you from the

noise which may be your affliction or pleasure, but he knows what is best for you. One of the great problems with noise is that it prevents us from facing home truths by drowning them out. We live under pressure for results, and that makes us impatient to work and make money. We are gregarious creatures, hungry for the company which easily threatens our time with God.

It's quiet in the desert. The wind may howl, whipping the sand into whirling storms which whistle in the sparse trees. The cries of the hunter and the hunted are shrill interruptions, and the sound of rare wildlife is a welcome interlude in nature's struggle for a patchy existence. Led into an eerie hush, you face a loneliness very different from the peaceful intimacy you enjoy alone on the top of a mountain, but God visits both places.

My first desert experience was the consequence of guilt, the guilt of murder. It isolated me from all company and froze me, even in the heat. You don't need sand for your desert which can be much nearer home, even home itself. In the unfamiliar quiet, God speaks to you, calling you to receive his mercy so that you can serve him again. There is no hiding place, however vast the wilderness, and there was none for me when he called. My discovery was that the voice of God changes the desert into a mountain, sometimes slowly, sometimes suddenly, but he changes it. In the desert, there is neither distraction nor confusion, and God deals powerfully with you. You feared an arid desert, but no place is dry when he is with you.

(4) The place of meeting

'Afterwards Moses and Aaron went to Pharaoh and said, "This is what the Lord, the God of Israel, says: 'Let my people go, so that they may hold a festival to me in the desert'"' (Ex 5:1).

Great men will give testimony to their desert meetings, and we were confident that we too could meet the

Lord. I may have been on the mountain when God called me (Ex 3:1–2), but I was also in the desert (Ex 3:1). 'At this, Moses hid his face, because he was afraid to look at God' (Ex 3:6). God does not abandon us in the wilderness, he leads us into a solitary place to achieve great things in us; the time in the desert has special meaning for his saving work. You can trace this in the experience of Israel, and you will do well to translate it into your own lives.

God has power to transform the desert, as the visions of future prophets will make clear. We are a practical people who don't think in abstract ways. We use blunt language, and our poets will produce vivid descriptions of the pictures the Lord gives them. They will see a future where the desert changes. The wilderness becomes a river; dry ground turns into flowing springs; vast spaces of barren land teem with well-fed people; wildlife enjoys peace with itself in new conditions of paradise, and flowers bloom in rich soil where formerly they eked out their lives in competition with marauding thistles. Creation celebrates its victory in dance, and the trees clap their hands in the exuberance we knew when we sang the Exodus song of freedom (Ex 15:1–18). No, you should not take the visions literally; yes, trees clapping their hands would look odd, but the vision meets your suffering and offers a mighty hope for your future. It is a picture of conditions which display the power of God.

My life has served up bitter moments, causing me one disappointment after another, and I shall not fulfil my great dream of entering Canaan. But I have not lost the impetus of my call. I have revelled in the mountains without shunning the desert, and I go peacefully to my grave with the original vision burning in me. A succession of prophets will vindicate my work, and believers as discerning as you will acknowledge me as the distinguished predecessor of those who speak for God.

Postscript

Shortly after he completed the final chapter, Moses died. In accordance with his wishes, he received a quiet burial in an unrecorded place. There was little fuss and no map was kept of his grave. The words 'Tell the Israelites to move on' (Ex 14:15), were engraved on his tomb, and immediately after appropriate mourning the people did move on. Moses had commissioned Joshua to succeed him, and the new leader gave clear instructions for the journey to continue.

'And Moses the servant of the Lord died there in Moab, as the Lord had said. He buried him in Moab, in the valley opposite Beth Peor, but to this day no one knows where his grave is. Moses was a hundred and twenty years old when he died, yet his eyes were not weak nor his strength gone. The Israelites grieved for Moses in the plains of Moab thirty days, until the time of weeping and mourning was over' (Deut 34:5–8). 'So Joshua ordered the officers of the people, "Go, through the camp and tell the people, 'Get your supplies ready. Three days from now you will cross the Jordan here to go in and take possession of the land the Lord your God is giving you for your own'"' (Josh 1:10–11).

I Am Joseph

by Alan Pain

You've heard all about his amazing Technicolour dreamcoat.

Now meet the star behind the stripes.

From slave in Egypt to Pharaoh's right-hand man, Joseph's meteoric rise to fame charts a story of family intrigue, murderous jealousy, sexual drama, incredible rescue, prophetic dreams, and final reconciliation.

'An imaginative and challenging first-person presentation and application of the exciting biblical adventure of Joseph.'

DAVID COHEN
General Director, Scripture Union

'Shows that yesterday's heroes have genuine relevance to today's generation. Packed with plenty of spiritual sting in the tail.'

CLIVE CALVER
General Director, Evangelical Alliance

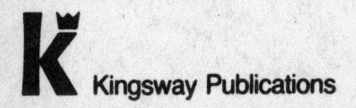

Kingsway Publications

I Am Jeremiah

by Alan Pain

Meet Jeremiah—the prophet who never wanted to be a prophet. Visionary of rotten figs, smasher of clay pots, and gate-crasher of His Majesty's banquet—wearing nothing but a cloak and a yoke.

From the stock to the docks, and the cell to the well, he was, as the saying goes, a 'right Jeremiah'.

Or was he?

This book penetrates beyond the doom and gloom to the heart of Jeremiah's message—a stark and heartbreaking one, yet carrying the promise of new hope. A message for our times.

'In a movingly personal yet humorous account, written as if by Jeremiah himself, Alan Pain paints a vivid but accurate word picture of one of the Old Testament's most colourful prophets. When you've read the book you'll want to read the Book.'

—**Derek Copley**
Principal, Moorlands Bible College

ALAN PAIN is Minister of Sutton Coldfield Baptist Church, a few miles outside Birmingham.

Kingsway Publications